A STROUD VALLEY
CHILDHOOD

Terry Jones
November 1992

A STROUD VALLEY
CHILDHOOD

Terry Jones

RADIO GLOUCESTERSHIRE

ALAN SUTTON

First published in the United Kingdom in 1992 by
Alan Sutton Publishing Limited
Phoenix Mill · Far Thrupp · Stroud · Gloucestershire
in association with BBC Radio Gloucestershire

First published in the United States of America in 1992 by
Alan Sutton Publishing Inc · Wolfeboro Falls · NH 03896–0848

British Library Cataloguing in Publication Data
A catalogue record for this book is available from the British Library

Library of Congress Cataloging in Publication Data applied for

Typeset in 9/13 Perpetua.
Typesetting and origination by
Alan Sutton Publishing Limited.
Printed in Great Britain by
The Bath Press, Bath, Avon.

Contents

List of Illustrations

Acknowledgements

The author and publisher would like to thank David Smith at Gloucestershire County Record Office for his help in supplying photographs. Those on pages 7, 38, 39 and 90 are reproduced courtesy of P.D. Turner.

Everything Quiet, Constable?

POLICE CONSTABLE JONES

I t's back to the days of hoops and hay carts, conkers and marbles, chips in newspaper and toast before the fire! But – let's start at the beginning, for me anyway. I was born in Gloucester way back in 1922. But I wasn't in Gloucester for long – about a year actually. I should probably have been there a little longer, if Father hadn't sung at the Police Concert.

You see – Father was a policeman.

A big, tall policeman. They were all big, tall policemen back in the 1920s. Nobody under 6 feet was even considered. They had two methods of moving about, namely walking and cycling. They pounded the beat or

Military policemen during the First World War. My father is seated second from right in the middle row

cycled to remote farms and stately homes, there to leave tickets (as they called them) to prove that they had been there.

There were no personal radios in those days. Once they were away from the Police Station – that was it. And, believe me, they preferred it that way, especially when homemade wine had to be tasted, resulting at times in great difficulty in remounting their heavy BSA bicycles!

They battled through storm or sweated through sunshine. They cycled and walked, and talked to poet and peasant, housewife and farmer, shop-keeper and schoolchildren. Everybody knew them and everybody liked them. They were big and solid, and a sign of safety and help.

But, to go back to the Police Concert. The reason why I was not in Gloucester for long was because of PC 97's enthusiastic performance there.

Northgate Street, Gloucester

This was the Gloucester my father patrolled as a young policeman in the 1920s

Father had a good singing voice, which really took off when primed by a couple of jars of Cheltenham Brewery's best bitter. And remember that back in 1923 beer was really beer.

Father had just rendered a great performance of 'Roses of Picardy', to tremendous applause from the Gloucestershire Constabulary's best bitter drinkers, and had been partaking of best bitter at a steady input himself. (The pints were being paid for by enthusiastic friends, so he was doing well.)

Across walked the chief constable and friend to congratulate the constable on his fine singing. (Father didn't quite remember what happened then, but was told about it by gleeful mates the next day.) It seems that, after the chief and friend had said 'Well done', PC 97 said 'Thank you, gentlemen' and backed up the thanks by tapping the chief constable's friend smartly on the head several times with the rolled up music sheet of 'Roses of Picardy'.

Thus followed banishment – to the wilds of the Forest of Dean. To Blakeney, to be exact!

Blakeney was a marvellous place in 1923. Quiet, mind you, with only two buses a week to Gloucester – Tuesdays and Saturdays.

According to Father, the house was dark and damp, with a stream at the bottom of the garden – a foul-smelling horror, in which swam rats as big as kittens.

We had a big black cat named Smut, who would grab these foul vermin in his mouth and proudly bring them into the kitchen for my mother, with all the pride of a farmer laying out his first fruits for the Harvest Festival.

To save my mother from a nervous breakdown, Authority relented, and we were moved to a small village named Oldland Common, not far from Bath. (The cat was bitterly disappointed and sulked for days.)

Childhood was a very happy time for me in the early 1930s. Long, hot summers, exciting snowy, frosty winters. Warm, lazy autumns and every spring heavy with buttercups in the fields and flowers of every description in the hedges.

Those April showers were even beautiful as well. Down came the rain for a while, sending up steam from the hot paths and roads. The showers only lasted a few minutes, whilst we youngsters used to huddle under the big oak in Farmer Dare's field, or in one of his nice, cosy barns.

Then, out we'd dash (whilst the sun and blue skies laughed out loud again), as we grabbed up the bats and balls, cycles and soapbox transport, and went on our way.

I suppose I was lucky with Father being a policeman in a safe job, when many men were out of work, but there wasn't much poverty about at Oldland Common. Everybody had big gardens and, in those days, everybody cared for each other. If Joe had beans in his garden, Jack didn't go hungry.

Claude's Grandma had a big pig at the bottom of her garden as well. We used to spend a lot of time down there. The pig fascinated us and sometimes we went into his sty to talk to him. I remember Claude slipped and sat down next to Percy the pig one day. His trousers were in a right state, I can tell you, and matters didn't improve when we arrived back in Grandma's kitchen for dinner. Ye Gods! Didn't he pong!

He finished up in the tin bath pretty quick, I remember that.

Of course, the day came when Percy was to be executed. What a dreadful row he made. You could hear it all over the village. 'Dreadful thing to do', old Mrs Hodges said. 'Cruel I call it.'

'Ah! Just you remember that, Mrs Hodges', said Butcher Barnes. 'I'll be sure I don't sell thee any bacon or lard when I have it in the shop. You wouldn't like to fry old Percy in the pan now, would yer?'

Funny thing – old Ma Hodges was always skipping over his sawdust floor as soon as the bacon arrived. 'What's done is done', she snapped. 'I'll take 2 pound of the best and a pound of lard.'

THE CONSTABLE AND THE INVALID CHAIR

The young policemen of Gloucester City in the late 1920s were sometimes like the Fourth Form at Will Hay's notorious 'Narkover College'. They were forever up to pranks against their fellow officers. One that sticks in my mind was really the limit and it was one that my father was particularly fond of.

PC George Towser was always happy to be on nightshift around the City.

*The ancient lock-up near the
Bear Inn, Bisley*

He would like to say to unsuspecting victims, 'What's copper nitrate?' and, when they said they just didn't know, he would bellow, 'What they pay me on the nightshift', and howl with laughter at his hilarious joke! George was that sort of gentleman.

Now, the reason he liked to be on nightshift (that's the 10 a.m. to 6 p.m. one) was because there was one house he had to pass with a big garden and summer house at the bottom. In the summer house was one of those old basket invalid chairs and George (with a couple of Cheltenham Brewery's 'Best in the West' in his big pockets), would creep down the garden path into the summer house and uncork the 'tipple', settle nicely in the old basket chair and soon would be fast asleep (after his little refreshment break).

He would be firm asleep till about 5.30 a.m., when he would lose the bottles somewhere, amble back to the Station, and inform the sergeant that 'All was quiet on the Gloucester Front'.

7

Now, a couple of the lads got to know about his little snooze in the summer house and, when they were next on nights with George, they plotted a deadly plot! Giving him plenty of time to go to sleep, they met up and crept down to the summer house.

It was a fine warm summer's night, as they carefully wheeled the sleeping officer, in his basket chair, down the path and out on to the main road. They knew nothing would wake George, short of an earthquake, once he'd had his usual 'Cheltenham'.

And, that is where they left him! Bang in the middle of the main road. And that is where he found himself when he woke up! He was absolutely furious. He had to creep back up the garden path, pushing the old chair back to the summer house, then get back to sign off. He couldn't say a word with the sergeant there and (of course) there were just greetings from the lads. 'Okay, George? Quiet night, George?'

If poor old George could have found the culprits there would have been attempted murder, I'm sure. Trouble was, he never could tell whether it was police or civilians who put him 'out to graze', as it were. But the whole Station got to know about it, as you can guess!

George always had nightmares after. (How many people passed by that night and wondered what a policeman was doing sitting in an old invalid chair firm asleep in the middle of the road? Alas, he never knew.)

'WE DO PUT OUR FOOT IN IT'

Back in the 1930s we had a dog. Not the one we had at Bisley, but nevertheless a most intelligent animal (much too intelligent in fact), which was brought sharply to the attention of my father one fine evening in the Forest of Dean, many moons ago.

Dad had a beat that took him to several small villages and hamlets, which in those days all boasted a pub, which had to be visited by PC 97 (without the knowledge of Authority, I might add). He always took the Airedale with him for company. On one particular night he wished he hadn't!

*Father on point duty in Stroud in the
1930s*

You see, this was the night Sergeant decided to accompany my father on his rounds. Dad was peeved. No visits to 'mine host' tonight along the way, there to sup a jar and yarn away the evening. Just plod, plod, plod.

So, off they started with the intelligent Airedale trotting ahead (his name was Bruce, by the way).

Soon they came to the first pub and the intelligent Airedale trotted ahead of them, down the garden path to the door and there he sat, tongue out, beaming all over his face, as only intelligent Airedales can.

Dad walked past with Sergeant, taking no notice of Bruce, as if he didn't exist. A few yards on he called back, 'Come on, Bruce. What d'you think you're doing?' Looking slightly bewildered, the dog trotted along behind.

The next village came in view. Up to the next village pub – and the performance was repeated. Down the path, tail wagging, outside the pub door, sitting and waiting.

9

Dad, feeling decidedly uncomfortable by now, once more called to his faithful friend. 'Come on boy, come on Bruce', and once more a decidedly reluctant Airedale came ambling behind them.

But it wasn't long before the next pub appeared and the dog was down the path to the door once more. Poor Dad didn't even call him this time. They walked on in a rather uneasy silence. Then spoke the mighty one. 'It seems, Jones, that this dog of yours is far more familiar with your check points than you are tonight!'

Father seemed doomed to put his foot into trouble though with sergeants.

A couple of years later he was stationed at Oldland Common, in the south of the county, and the sergeant there looked as if he had just come off the Army parade ground. He was a stiff disciplinarian, bald headed, with a waxed moustache. He was every inch the man in charge.

He had five constables under him and ruled them with a rod of iron. (It's hard to believe this now, but he actually had them on a rota washing the living quarters' floors, as well as the guardroom.) They were 'domestics', as well as 'law keepers'.

Of course, old Albert was on a good number and you might wonder why the young policemen didn't complain to headquarters. Well, the reason was Kathy, the gorgeous daughter of Sergeant Albert Brown. (How such an ugly old so-and-so could have had such a super daughter was always an unsolved mystery in the village – but there it was.)

You see – in those days girls didn't go out to work so much as they do today. Kathy worked at the Police Station helping her mother with the running of the home. She was about 18 at the time. So the lads quite enjoyed cleaning up the floors and steps and shaking the mats, because they could chat up Kathy *and* there was a great, big bonus – Mrs Brown made cakes that melted in the mouth.

Also, both the ladies were on the side of the young policemen – so much so that, when Sergeant Albert Brown walked out on to his daily beat to check up on things and assure the good folk of Oldland that all was well, there would be a long tea break with Mrs Brown, Kathy, tea and cakes.

Not only did the 'cleaners' have their little cakes, but it was always a must for any constable out on the beat to sneak back to the Station and join in the 'happy hour', as it were.

Now, on a particular sunny morning, my father wended his way back at around 10 a.m. and poked his head around the kitchen door. 'Hello, Kath', he yelled. 'Has the bald-headed old "Walrus" gone yet?'

A deep, dark and dusky growl came from behind the high-back kitchen seat. 'The old "Walrus" has not gone yet, Jones. Get out on your beat at once!'

Poor old Dad. Albert was a late starter that morning. Everybody was in the dog-house. The one who got the most flak was poor Mrs Brown and it was the end of those 'exceedingly good cakes' for the law officers. No more fraternizing with the staff after that.

It's strange how people said things, either to, or near Dad in the 1930s, that were meant to be serious, but which turned out to be very funny.

Take the day when he was on point duty in Stroud – those crossroads where Gloucester Street, King Street and Lansdown meet are still very tricky, even with High Street now a pedestrian area.

A lot of heavy transport used to come up the pitch in those days and a policeman was always on duty to hold up all traffic in order to give the climbing vehicles right of way, especially the big lorries. Stop them on that slope and they would have one heck of a job to start up again.

A huge lorry was coming up and Dad gave him the 'all clear', signalling to people not to cross the road outside of W. H. Smith, because the lorry had to really belt up and come around the blind bend at a fair old lick.

All went well until there was a frightful screech of brakes and a torrent of curses from the driver. Dad went quite pale and hurried across. There, standing in the middle of the road, was a little man in spectacles, dressed in black and carrying a large wreath. The bonnet of the huge lorry was about a foot from his face.

The lorry driver, having exhausted his lurid vocabulary, delivered his final shot. 'And I'll tell you this, "Lightning". If you don't look where you're going in future, you'll need that nice big wreath for yourself.'

BISLEY — HAM AND EGGS

'That dog', said my father, 'will have to go.' 'That dog' was a small, black animal. His mother was a pure-bred Scottie, but — well, the pure-bred Scottie went 'walkies' one fine day. The result of her unladylike behaviour was two small, black offspring that were definitely not 'pure-bred Scottie'.

The owner, who lived in Eastcombe, near Stroud (desperate to get rid of her well-groomed bitch's indiscretion), sold the offspring off quickly for 10 shillings each. My father bought one (much to the delight of his two small sons and wife), but he was not so happy about the deal once the animal became part of the family.

This is the 'shoplifter of Bisley', partial to ham and eggs, at his new home at Cashes Green, 1935

The year was 1934, the place – the Police Station, Bisley. Not where it is these days, but down near the church lich-gates at Sinegar House – the name is still engraved high up on the side of the house. Father was officer-in-charge, a position of great importance for PC 97 of the Gloucestershire Constabulary. So important, in fact, that he was supplied with a huge BSA bicycle. 'Stand up and beg' bikes, we called them. Huge monsters. If they fell over it took two men to lift them up again.

To assist Father to cycle around the wilds of Bisley in the 1930s in the dark, the BSA was equipped with an acetylene lamp. One lit this thing by putting into its base a quantity of rock-like material (calcium carbide), pouring water on it to produce a gas which, when lit, gave out a brilliant, white light. The smell was appalling until the thing got going.

The duty of the BSA night patrol was to catch poachers. Father never caught any. A steady light on a slow-moving cycle at night could only mean

Bisley High Street as it was in the 1930s – not a car in sight. There was a post office then, on the left, and the police station is further down, by the tree on the right

one thing to the Poaching Club – 'Here comes old Bobby Jones'. ('Look lively and clear off away from the light.')

The local gentry would complain to the police and Father would dutifully write it all down. Rabbits were poached again. 'Right-oh, sir! I'll be out there tonight.'

It was quite the thing to see gentlemen cycling around Bisley in those days with rabbits tied to their handlebars visiting the houses and often meeting PC 97 on his duty. 'Missus like a nice fresh rabbit for dinner, Mr Jones? Only a bob.' It was pointless asking where they came from. My father jolly well knew where they came from. Oh, it was quite a game, believe me!

But – I stray from the central character – this dog. He had bad habits, picked up from his wandering dad, no doubt. He was a gifted thief. But not a selfish one. He seemed to think his mission in life was to supply the people who lived in the Police Station with free breakfasts.

Opposite us was the local Post Office and General Store. Every morning, as soon as the shop was open, the dog would enter the place, grab an egg out of the egg basket and bring it back into our kitchen and deposit it on the mat – always in perfect condition! Not so much as a crack. He was so small, he used to come in (below eye level as it was) and do the deed.

My mother just couldn't begin to understand where the eggs came from. Mind you, he rationed us out – only one a day.

Mother figured out he must have found these eggs in the hedges some-where. It was all free range those days and the 'old biddies' would often lay their eggs in hedges, much to the annoyance of their owners.

But, there came a day when the good lady over at the Post Office came over to report to the Law that her eggs were being stolen. Even at one a day, the total was adding up. Dad wrote down all the particulars, with a queer feeling mounting in his stomach. It didn't need Stroud CID to figure out how far he would have to go to apprehend the culprit.

He assured the good lady that all would be well. He would do his duty.

When, later on, he walked into our kitchen, he found Mother sitting down in her wooden chair looking quite pale. 'Vic', she gasped, 'he never found that in a field.' There, with tail wagging – pleased as punch – was our

The police station, Bisley, where Dad was Officer in Charge from 1933 to 1935

pet animal standing behind a cooked ham as big as himself. How he got it out of the shop, goodness knows.

This is why my father was saying, 'That dog will have to go.' It took some courage for PC 97 to return a nice big cooked ham to the Post Office and General Stores and tell the staff he had found the thief (his own, well- trained police dog!) Of course, he had to pay for all the stolen food. My brother and I nearly had hysterics – so did the rest of Bisley, when word got around.

Of course, our lovable black criminal didn't leave us. But he was imprisoned from then on (on a big, strong lead). It gave the Poaching Club such a laugh that Bert Jackson gave me a beautiful, big rabbit. 'Here, young Terry. Take this 'un to yer Mum.'

Lovely dinner we had the next day and the little black thief had a good helping too.

15

The Arrival of the 'Empress Josephine'

N ow, what about this visit to Bisley by royalty? Well – it was the only time I saw my Grandmother laugh, till tears formed in her eyes. It all started when a strange, well-dressed middle-aged woman appeared in the square where the pub is. All of us youngsters were on holiday and she proved to be a star attraction. Where she had come from, goodness knows, but she spoke very posh; and informed us all that she was 'Josephine, Empress of France'.

That was enough for the kids. They revelled in it! Soon the adults started to gather. 'Take me to the Palace! you peasants', she shouted. 'How dare you insult your Empress!' (Well, even the adults were close to tears of laughter by now.)

Of course, it was becoming obvious that she was 'off her trolley', so some of the more responsible citizens decided to take her to the Police Station and let Dad take her in hand. Now, that's when she started to struggle and get agitated, so a couple of youngsters cut off down to our place to inform Dad what was happening.

It so happened that he had already had a phone call from a private mental home a few miles away, to ask him to look out for one of their patients who had wandered off. 'She was a very "uppercrust" lady, and perfectly harmless,' they said, 'but was quite convinced she was Josephine, Empress of France.'

So, of course, when the news reached him about the strange lady up in the square, Father knew who it was.

Buttoning up his tunic and ramming his helmet firmly on his head, he rolled with stately gait up to the scene of all the excitement.

'All right – stand back everybody', demanded the Law. They gave way and Dad confronted the strange lady. 'She'll kick up a fuss, Mr Jones, if you touch her', said those who had tried. 'All right,' said Dad. 'Leave this to me!'

He saluted the lady politely. 'Your Highness,' he said, 'I have been dispatched by the Emperor Napoleon to escort you to my chateau – there to await the carriage of His Highness to take you on your journey to his palace.'

The gracious lady gazed at PC 97, gazed at the peasants (in near hysterics by then) and, as good as gold, said 'Thank you, my man, pray lead the way!' So, off they went to the Police Station, followed by an admiring crowd.

Dad took her into our front room, where Grandma and Mother and my young brother were having a cup of tea. (I was in like a shot as well. I wasn't going to miss this one.) 'The Empress, I am sure, would like a cup of tea', said the old Dad (bowing like he was rehearsing for the next Women's Institute production of *The Merry Widow*).

'Indeed, yes', said the posh lady. And so she did, whilst Dad phoned up the home, and told them to come and fetch their patient.

When they arrived, our lady had already reduced my Grandmother to laughter, as I stated earlier on. She had been telling us what a difficult time she had with 'Old Nap' sometimes, when his eye strayed to other ladies.

She thanked us all very much for our hospitality to one so regal and trotted out to Napoleon's 'coach', with the two medical men 'bowing' her in.

'Thanks, Officer, for your tact and clever handling of our patient', they said. 'As long as we treat her as Josephine, she's no trouble. Thank goodness you knew what to do. You'd never have got her to come any other way!' So, off they went – and that was that!

Grandma couldn't stop laughing for hours after. In fact, we all had a good laugh that afternoon.

'But, Dad,' I wanted to know, 'how come you hit on the idea to tell the lady Napoleon had sent for her?' 'Ah!', said the Law, with a twinkle in his eye, 'I wasn't that clever. They told me on the phone to just tell her Napoleon had sent me. If I didn't, wild horses wouldn't have got her to move.'

So ended the event when royalty visited Bisley in the early 1930s.

THE EVILS OF DRINK

There were ever-present temptations set before our noble officers (who kept the peace in the 1930s), to sample a glass of ale or a tipple of homemade wine during (or off) duty.

My father and his fellow police officers always counted the cost (as it were) at the end of the day, as to how they had resisted the temptation to partake whenever the opportunity arose. They were always happy to report that they had all failed. They all had their little places to check that – 'Everything all right, sir?'

Mind you, the homemade wine these farmers made around Stroud in those days was lethal. Put some in your cigarette lighter and you'd lose your eyebrows!

But, for sheer planning, it would have been hard to beat old Charlie Skinner down at Cashes Green. Now Charlie was a 'cider man' and the kids used to call him 'Cider Charlie'.

He could really sink 'scrumpy' and no mistake. He used to say, 'When I go – Bulmers go!'

He'd retired from the police, which was just as well. Every morning he used to cycle up to the local and sit there till closing time, sampling the apple.

Then, when he was ready to go, a few of his mates would help him onto his bike and launch him (so to speak), like helpers in a cycle race. He used to live in the Crescent, and would cycle round and round the houses until his missus and teenage daughter saw him. Then, out they would come and catch him as he cycled by. (Somehow it all reminded me of the 'Royal Mail basket' on the side of the railway line, that would catch the mail from the express train going by, in those days.)

It was always successful after a while, but Charlie had to make the circuit more than once sometimes when they missed him. You can imagine the yells of advice that used to come from the juvenile population – 'Go it Charlie! That was too fast! Next time round Charlie!' – then the loud cheers when poor Mrs Skinner and her daughter finally made a catch and hauled him back home. I feel sorry for the two women (looking back with hindsight), but way back then we all thought it was the show of the day.

The 10 p.m. to 6 a.m. shift was the most popular in Stroud town for the police, which was strange on the face of it. But, when I explain that one of the security checks was the Stroud Brewery, maybe the light will begin to flicker in.

PC Victor Jones in the late 1930s, off duty in Stroud with his trusty BSA

It was surprising the number of checks that had to be made on the brewery. By the side of those huge vats of beer sat the police nightshift (all two of them).

The brewery men would just dip their pint pots into this magnificent brew (and it was of a terrific strength because it hadn't been diluted for the public consumption yet). Then, of course, the police force would also dip a pint pot into the brew, and a good time was had by all.

What always used to amuse Dad was that the brewery boys would be supping booze all night (whilst working), then, when their meal break came, they would open up a flask of tea!

Mother would always know where Dad had been when he came home just after 6 a.m. 'Your father has been around that brewery again. He's talking too much.'

Dad told me years later that the patrol man dropped in once (after parking his police car in a discreet spot) and joined in the 'hop sampling'. He wasn't used to it and, to cut the story short, one of them had to drive him back to the Police Station (whilst Dad held him upright), and the two of them had to hold him up and guide his hand when he signed off!

(Stroud Brewery is no more, but I have to have a smile every time I pass the site where it used to be.)

But, there was one of those mighty men who beat all the others when he'd had a drop too much. That was old 'Banger' Barnes. 'Banger' had a vocabulary of colourful language that was a schoolboy's delight, and it was always extra loud and colourful when 'Banger' got excited.

There was a certain afternoon in Stroud in the late 1930s (1939, I think it was). Anyway – a 'sweet young thing' in an MG sports car was having trouble getting her vehicle turned round in one of Stroud's narrow streets. An interested crowd was gathering and the sweet, very posh, young thing was suffering!

Up comes 'Banger', full of confidence and 'Stroud Brewery'. 'All right Miss – back her! No, no – not that way! No, no! Get her ass round.' (The sweet young thing blushed crimson and the car seemed doomed to stay jammed across the road for ever.) 'Look Miss,' said 'Banger', 'drive her out again. Right! – now in, but get her ass right round – that's right! Strewth – women drivers!' The MG and the sweet young thing finally made it and disappeared, leaving 'Banger' red in the face.

Two days later 'Banger' had to present himself at the inspector's office in Stroud. 'Ah, Barnes', said the mighty one. 'I've had a complaint from a young woman. She objects to the rear of her car being described as its ass. Three days' suspension without pay, Barnes! Out you go.'

Poor old 'Banger'. As he was going out, the inspector said, 'By the way, that complaint came via Cheltenham HQ. If you must use your strange language to motorists, make sure next time it isn't the daughter of one of our HQ bigwigs, for goodness sake!'

A PIPE AND NIGHT MAIL 'NOSH'

Without a doubt, some strange things used to happen to the country bobby long ago, when he tramped his lonely beat through the hours of darkness. But my mate told me one the other week that takes some beating.

Old Charlie was stationed in Cirencester in the 1940s and, like all the other lads, used to find the night patrol a bit of a drag, especially around the town. There wasn't much to do apart from trying the doors of shops to see that they were locked. (Around 2 a.m. in those days, breaking the law wasn't on.) So all was very quiet.

Most of the policemen whiled away the lonely night by having a cigarette on the go and, if anybody came along, it was easy to hide it in the palm of your hand, or, if it was a superior officer come to check up on you, you could drop the thing and grind it out.

But Charlie had a problem here. Charlie was a 'pipe man'. He didn't like cigarettes but, my word, he enjoyed his old pipe. But, as I said, there was a problem. What does one do with a pipe when someone comes along? You can't hide that in the palm of your hand, or drop it.

So, Charlie spent some time during the lonely hours thinking this one out. He couldn't put it in his uniform pockets, because they were not designed to take pipes. Baton, yes, handcuffs, yes, notebook, likewise, but pipes, definitely no!

Then, one night, a great idea hit him. There was one untapped available space. His policeman's helmet. So he got to work back home. He designed and fitted a little wire rack in his helmet (still leaving plenty of space for his head). This rack just held his pipe a treat.

From then on Charlie puffed away contentedly on duty, night and day, because as soon as he got to some remote spot on day duty it was OK and, when he saw someone coming, out of his mouth came his pipe, a short tap on his helmet and up inside out of the sight in the little pipe rack. 'Good afternoon, Officer.' 'Good afternoon, sir' (all very correct).

But the best of plans misfire, and misfire this one did, with the emphasis on the 'fire'.

One dark and dreary night Charlie was standing in a doorway in Cirencester, puffing away with the world at peace, when suddenly, about a dozen yards away up draws the police patrol car and out gets the inspector (of all people). It was just the sergeant as a rule who checked that things were OK.

Charlie, in a panic, tore off his helmet and jammed his old briar in the rack, replacing it just in time, when the inspector bore down on him. 'Ah,

The old police station where Dad worked in the 1930s and 1940s

Brown', said the Great One. 'Just thought I'd come along tonight and spend a little time with you. Everything quiet?' 'Oh, yes, sir', said Charlie. 'Just checking the doors, sir.' 'Good man, good man. Well, let's have a walk around then.'

So, off they went along Cricklade Street. It wasn't long before the inspector looked at Charlie with quite a curious gaze. A little later, another gaze. By the time they reached the junction with Lewis Lane, the inspector was getting quite alarmed. 'Are you all right, Brown?' 'All right? Yes, Sir!' ('Hmmm.')

Along Watermoor Road they walked. A second question. 'Are you all right, Brown?' (Charlie was beginning to wonder if the inspector had been sampling the grape before his spell of duty.) 'Yes sir, quite all right.'

22

Then, finally, the inspector stopped. 'Brown', he said, 'if you are all right – then *please* put my mind at rest – and tell me, why is smoke coming out of the air-vents of your helmet?'

Oh dear! In his panic, our Charles hadn't tapped out his pipe and it was going away in fine style in his helmet!

A veil really must be drawn over the painful scene that followed, but I'd be willing to wager that many a friend of the inspector laughed his head off when he told them about his policeman with a helmet that smoked!

Over in Stroud in those far-off days, my own father, PC 97, found a very different way to pass the nightshift away. Of course, there was the Brewery check, which I have previously mentioned, but there was also the nightmail, which glided into Stroud Station in the small hours.

Headed by a gleaming green 'Castle', hissing like some huge kettle, the sight of it on a clear, frosty night was a joy to the old Dad. But, there was an added bonus. The drivers and firemen all knew him and, as the mail was being loaded and unloaded, they would help him into the warm cab, while they got the coal shovel ready for breakfast.

Yes! Into the blazing boiler fire went the shovel. 'More hygienic than your kitchen frying pan', they used to say. Then, on to the shovel the eggs were cracked and the sausages were dropped and the bacon was slid. One glorious, sizzling sound and a beautiful, mouthwatering smell, then it was on to an enamel plate. Dad was given a corner to sit in and they used to share their 'nosh-up' with him.

A strange sight, surely – a big policeman washing down his eggs, bangers and bacon with a nice real cup of tea (in a real enamel cup too), together with the driver and fireman on the footplate of a huge, record-breaking 'GWR Castle' locomotive.

It was all over too soon. The guard was blowing his whistle. The constable clambered back down on to the platform. The huge living 'powerhouse' of metal and steam blew its whistle (a wonderful sound on the night air) and they were away down the line to Gloucester.

Dad used to stand and watch until the red light on the guard's van disappeared around the bend and decided that there were times when it wasn't too bad being a policeman on the 10 a.m. to 6 p.m. nightshift!

Wolf Pack and Hay Cart
up Bisley Way

The Bisley Wolf Pack

In the year 1933, in the village of Bisley near Stroud, it was felt among certain of the population that it would be nice if Bisley formed its own branch of the Boy Scouts. A junior branch, it would be known as the 'Wolf Cubs'.

Why Wolf Cubs, goodness knows. But it was certainly a good name for the band of hopefuls who (rather against their better nature) arrived at the first meeting in a converted garage at the bottom of one of the wealthy families' gardens on a bright, summer's evening.

The garden belonged to the Talbots, a very well-respected family in the village, due to the fact that they had 'oodles of boodle' and two cars. Their place was like a National Heritage property, like you see on those big, glossy calendars. So it was natural for the good citizens of Bisley to approach Anthony Talbot, the one and only son (aged about 26), and ask him if he would get permission and then take charge of the 'Bisley Cubs'.

Young Mr Talbot was delighted to be offered such a post and got the necessary wheels turning, so that he was 'in all his glory' soon as Cub master.

Had he been able to look into the future at that point he would probably have looked for a job in the north of England as a way of politely declining such a position of trust. But alas for young Mr Talbot, such things were not possible.

My father and mother were delighted to hear of the formation of something like law and order for the under-12s, and (having blissful thoughts of days free of irritable folk stamping into the Police Station with complaints about being drenched by water pistols, bowled over by runaway car tyres, narrowly escaping hospital treatment by just dodging in time out of the way of brakeless wooden trucks on pram wheels, and greenhouse windows with large holes in them caused by a cricket ball landing in the middle of their best cucumbers) decided that I should be a noble Wolf Cub, together with my 'junior disturbers of the peace'.

So (as I have already mentioned), there we all were one bright evening.

Now when I tell you that young Anthony Talbot was the spitting image of the brilliant Frank Williams who took the part of the vicar in *Dad's Army* on the TV, you can guess that he was going to have trouble with us straight away. He already had his uniform, complete with long shorts (if that sounds daft, well they did actually almost come to his knees).

Then there was his Scouts' lanyard and kerchief around his neck, nicely brought together on his chest with his wooden 'woggle'.

He did look a sketch and Percy whispered to me right away, 'I think I'm going to enjoy being a Cub. He's asking for it.' I was all in agreement. Poor old Anthony was fair game.

So (clapping his hands together) Anthony said, 'Well, come along you young chaps and let's get to know each other and get you all nicely into your new patrols and all be nice, friendly young Cubs together. What! What!'

As some of our gang's enemies had assembled as well as us (due to their mum's sending them out of harm's way for an evening), 'nice and friendly' was the last thing we had in mind.

Now, the first thing to be done was, of course, to get us all into two little groups as patrols. That was asking for it straight away. It was a case of 'them and us' from the word go.

Then, after being measured for our green jerseys, black trousers and green caps (to come later) it was a case of 'to business' and that was learning to tie knots. That got awfully boring until Percy found out that if you got a reef knot nice and big in a loop of thin rope you couldn't half give the enemy a good wallop with it.

He practised it on old Fatty Davies as he was bending over to pick up his $\frac{1}{2}$ pence sherbert fountain he had just dropped, and the yell that proceeded from the large one brought the Cub master hurrying over to see what was the trouble.

'He's belted me on the [well, I'll use the word "bottom" here, but Bisley youth didn't use that word, I can assure you, when referring to their posterior!].'

'Now, boys, no larking about', bleated young Mr Talbot. There was quietness after, but, as everybody was busy getting whopping great reef knots ready, it looked as if the first meeting was going to be most interesting.

Well, despite the warlike tension between the dear little Cubs, there were some times when a truce was declared. This was due to bribery rather than a sense of duty, mind you, on the part of the ever-nervous young Mr Talbot.

After one particularly hectic afternoon out 'on location' as it were, Mr Talbot had news for us. It was supposed to have been a tracking game. One patrol had to disappear into the wilds, leaving clues to be followed up, and the rest of the gentle Cubs had to find 'em.

Actually, the afternoon ended with two of us falling out of a tree, four going nutting instead (lots of super hazelnuts around Bisley in those days) and another crowd ending up in a dust-up with Doreen Harris and her mob of 'girl rural jungle fighters'. They started hurling insults at us. 'Dear little boys in their dear little jerseys and nice little trousers. Did Mummy wash your little faces for you and make you nice and clean for nice Mr Talbot?'

So they had to be upended into the mud by the side of Old Marshall's Pond. (The side the cows used the most.) I went home smelling to the high skies because I skidded on a cow dab and landed on my backside wallop on the next one. (I had to disrobe outside by the gooseberry bushes, I remember, before Mum would let me indoors.)

Mr Talbot's news was that we were all invited to his huge house and gardens by his mother, where we were all to enjoy a game of croquet with some little friends of hers from Cheltenham.

The mind boggles! Croquet – what, us? Walking around a silly old lawn with silly old mallets knocking silly old balls through silly old hoop things (we'd seen dear Mrs Talbot tottering around the lawn with some very refined people at different times engaged in this breathless, nerve-tingling excitement and the thought of it appalled us).

'Sorry, Mr Talbot,' said Arthur, 'I can't come. Have to go out with Mum.' 'Nor me', I yelped. 'Nor me, Mr Talbot.' The chorus of voices grew.

'So sorry, lads', smiled Anthony. 'There's tea on the lawn afterwards. Mother's homemade currant cake, you know. Cold ham and chicken, eggs and sausages, oh – and I nearly forgot – ice-cream and jelly and jam tarts. Never mind! Our little Cheltenham friends will no doubt be able to cope with the extra load.'

Our faces dropped. We suddenly decided our mums would prefer us to support the Cubs meeting for croquet after all.

It was a glorious afternoon and evening, with a super spread on the lawn *and* we managed to trip up the Cheltenham swank-pots several times with our little croquet mallets, so it wasn't boring after all.

GIRLS

I t's now time to look at the 'fair sex' (if one can call them that when one recalls childhood days as I'm doing). I think the 'unfair sex' would be a better description when we were young. In our gang we had Fred and Alan, who always had our deepest sympathy. You see – these two unfortunate 11 year olds were struggling with terrible burdens. They both had elder sisters.

Now, elder sisters were 'the end'. Younger sisters were bad enough, but you could have pram races with them when your mother made you wheel them out for a ride. I sometimes wonder how any little girls lived to be big girls after the number of tumbles they had when a couple of push-chairs collided on the last 10 yards to the finishing line. But they did and a bullseye or two used to stop them squealing after they were dusted down and set upright again.

But, elder sisters – they just did nothing but tell your mother about everything. 'I'll tell our Mam', seemed to be the limit of their vocabulary. They just had no sense! How could an Apache chief lead his band on a surprise attack on the white settlers without getting dirt on his knees? If his trousers got torn scaling the castle at Nottingham, or he walked with a limp after falling off Walt Simmonds's pile of boxes down the coalyard whilst engaging in the final shoot-out with Al Capone's mob, excuses for mothers were 'I fell down, Mum', or 'There was a nail sticking out of Alec's gatepost, Mum', and that was that. Until big sister got into the act. 'They were up that duckpond again after you told them not to go.' 'They were on Walt Simmonds's boxes again. The ones that aren't safe to get on.' 'They were down by the railway track, Mum.'

It was awful. There was nothing we could do about it. Sundays were dreadful. We had to dress in our Sunday best and go to tea at their homes. It would have been super if it was just us lads. We could have had wrestling matches in the garden if it was fine, or plot future attacks on the rival gangs if it were wet.

Instead we had to sit and listen to girls narrating poems and singing 'Hark, Hark the Lark' and 'Come Where My Love Lies Bleeding', or some such awful thing. Then it was 'Time we had a haircut' and 'You've dropped peaches on your trousers three times in ten minutes'.

The additional problem was that some of them were so tough too. They were no cringing violets who we could creep up on and upend them in a cow dab. No fear.

I remember one blonde 'butch' about 12 years old, at Bisley. She was really well built and looked about 16.

We used to bait her young brother. He was only about 8 (real little gents we were). He used to sit in a little shed at the bottom of his garden doing something or other, so we would throw stones at the shed until he came raging out screaming at us and throwing great clods of earth at us.

It was great fun. We would catch him and shove grass down his trousers. He then used to start bawling and run home to tell his mum, leaving us hooting with laughter.

But, one day, things went very wrong. 'Young brother' was about to become a 'grass carrier' again, when out of the back gate hurtled the blonde Amazon.

She tore into the lot of us, delivering swipes left, right and centre and, boy, did she pack a punch. We scattered (the whole mob of us) – except poor old Percy. She grabbed him, chucked him on to the field face down and sat on him. Then she proceeded to bang his head into Old Harker's best mowing grass, with Percy yelling for mercy.

We couldn't abandon the poor soul, so we all turned back and grabbed the 12-year-old Amazon and dragged her off him. Old Mrs Harris was cycling by on her BSA at the time.

'How dare you boys attack that poor little girl', she screeched. 'Let her go or I'll go straight down to the Police Station.' (I groaned aloud. Not another complaint. There were too many coming in lately.)

We let her go. At least she had been dragged off Percy. She stuck out her tongue at us, hacked me on the shin and, taking her dear little brother with her, went and thanked Old Ma Harris for rescuing her!

After that the 'young hopeful' used to hurl turfs at us at every opportunity and, if we made a move to attack him, he'd yell out, 'I'll tell my sister, I'll tell my sister.'

Gathering miserably up at Harker's barn, we used to console ourselves with imagining a 'Superworld without Girls'. What possible use were they to anybody?

We even had to let them play in our cricket matches, or we would get no Saturday pennies.

Mind you, there was one exception. Her name was Molly. She saved the match against Oakridge one fine day. She was 11 years old and came out to keep 'slips' in her new High School uniform. There was a little terror we couldn't get out. He was smacking our bowlers all over the place. Then suddenly it happened.

Just as 'hopeful' leapt out to smash another boundary, demure little Molly lifted her new High School dress waist high, displaying her new High School knickers to his startled gaze! He never saw the ball. There was a crash of wickets and a delighted yell from us all, 'At last!'

Molly just stood there, all innocence, dress back in place. Only a few of us saw Molly's great fighting spirit. The batsman yelled 'It's not fair!' 'What's not fair?' He was beaten – what could he say?

After that, we thought we had better put Molly back in the pavilion to be scorer instead.

SCHOOLDAYS

School in the 1930s was a far cry from schools today, because there were no comprehensives back then. Once you reached the age of 12 the boys went to boys' school and girls went to girls' school, and you just made eyes at each other from your respective boundaries. Or you passed notes through the railings to your heart-throb (rather like feeding monkeys at the zoo). The mere idea of teenage boys and girls in the same classroom was unheard of.

Perhaps it was just as well. We learnt very little as it was. Females in our midst would have been even more of a distraction.

My brother and me at the entrance to Bisley police station in 1934

'Twas in the spring of 1934 I gave my parents quite a shock. Dad was officer-in-charge at the Police Station at Bisley at the time when I burst in to tell them the startling news that I had passed for Marling. Up to then my only sign of intelligence was that I knew every dance band playing on the wireless, every dance tune played, every film on at the Stroud Gaumont, every film star in every film and the exact days when the *Wizard*, *Hotspur*, *Rover*, *Funny Wonder*, *Magnet* and *Gem* came out.

Instead of saying 'Well done, son', Dad said 'It isn't possible. How on earth did he manage it?', 'he' being the village headmaster. From that day on Father looked upon the headmaster of our little village school as if he was some kind of superman.

Well, quite frankly, so did all the other parents because there were eight of us boys and girls, and none of us showed any sign of a desire to learn.

But our Headmaster was a genius. He just had to be able to dispatch his dear little children down to Marling and High. He knocked the three Rs (reading, 'riting and 'rithmatic) into us. He whacked us with his 'flexible friend' every time we got anything wrong. His 'flexible friend' was a nice, long ash plant and we got that cane across our hands so many times we just had to turn out clever enough for the grammar schools, whether we liked it or not.

There was an awful amount of snobbery in those days among the schools. Marling was top school, together with the Girls' High School. Then came the two Central Schools, which educated those who couldn't quite reach the required exam marks needed for Marling and High.

So, as soon as I knew I'd passed for Marling, it was down to old Bateman's shop in Stroud to get the gear so I could strut around Bisley and let everybody know what a clever little beast I was. Mother proudly watched her offspring strutting around even before the autumn term began. Mind you, Marling really did have a swank uniform – blue blazer with royal blue braid on the lapels and sleeves, and a big blue lion with 'M.S.' under it on the breast pocket.

Then there was the cap. A thing of pride was that cap. It was navy blue with royal blue stripes around it and that lion again on the front with the famous 'M.S.'.

Standard I and II Classes, Bisley School, around 1934. The headmaster who got us all through the scholarship to Marling High School is in the centre. My brother is on his left

It's a great shame they phased out schoolboy caps. They looked very smart, like cricketers, and especially if one was a prefect at Marling. Their lion on the front was golden instead of blue. How's that for swank? Those prefects didn't walk – they marched like Army officers.

When I got there, I was never particularly bright at school. By the time I reached the notorious 'fourth form' I had achieved a position of twenty-ninth at the end-of-term exams, out of a class of thirty-two. Father didn't look too happy when he read my reports. (It was usually 'Should try harder' after each subject.)

But there was one subject I was good at and that was English composition. I had a vivid mind and a racing pen (fed, no doubt, by dozens of visits to the Stroud Gaumont Cinema), and I could belt out some good stuff for a youngster. But I went over the top one day.

I always had a *Magnet* in my desk. This weekly magazine (featuring the adventures of the famous Billy Bunter and Greyfriars School) fitted just right between the desk top and the main section of the desk. While masters droned on I was away at Greyfriars down on the cricket field, or rowing up the river, or being chased by wild Chinamen or savage natives. (Small wonder I came twenty-ninth in the exams.)

But this particular day the English master set us a task to write an essay on any subject we chose. I opened my desk for my exercise book and there was the old *Magnet*, of course.

A flash of inspiration! Copy some of the professional stuff from the magazine and just change the names of the characters. So, with great care, I copied out a sizeable chunk and was very proud of it.

What I didn't realize was that the author, Frank Richards, was the most brilliant writer of school stories in the world.

When the essays were handed back to us the next week the English master had written all across the bottom of my masterpiece in red ink 'You are either a genius, or an inspired copyist' and he awarded me four marks out of ten (I suppose that was for trying).

But I loved school life way back then – especially the school dances. The stewards used to put down French chalk on the dance floor so that we could glide around better. We glided around all right, especially on some corners where there was too much chalk. We'd land up on the floor. Mind you, the boys used to enjoy sprawling all over the girls. The young ladies didn't like it though, especially when you all started to sneeze from the chalk up your nose. It was supposed to be 'slow, slow, quick-quick, slow' to Victor Silvester – usually it was 'slow, slow (atishoo, atishoo) slow' instead.

At the end of the dance it looked like we were all wearing tennis shoes. Yes, schooldays were, without doubt, very happy days for many of us.

HAYFIELDS AND HAY CARTS

It was quite a pleasant sight coming back over the Cotswolds the other week. All those fields of hay. Yet, something was not quite right. Those cubes of hay were all very neat and tidy. Too neat – too tidy!

My mind was racing again – way back to those wonderful 1930s, and me and our hayfields!

Yes, not the farmer's hayfields, but *our* hayfields. For (right from the time when those magnificent, great shire-horses moved in pulling the grass cutters across the fields and laying the grass all loose and flat behind them to the final ride on the hay cart) it was our territory.

We were all ages from 6 to 14 (boys and girls) in one whooping gang all looking forward to 'the season' with just as much excitement as any racegoer.

You see, within a couple of days, the grass would be turning to hay and great battles would be fought as huge loads of hay were grabbed up and used to belt each other or trip each other up into the super-smelling softness. (When I come to think of it – the dust must have been terrific, but I can't remember any of us having hay fever.)

Having tipped all the little girls headfirst into the piles of hay (by a simple procedure of catching hold of their ankles and lifting), it was time for us men to get down to the more serious business – the building of hay houses.

This was done by gathering lots of hay into circles and gradually building up these hay walls until they were like a stockade. Different gangs built different houses in different parts of the field. Oh, very busy we all were! When we finished the 'Tribal Wars' began. Raiding Apache braves whooping in! The object was to demolish the rivals' hay houses and carry away their squaws! That's where the girls came in. They were the squaws.

Central School girls were the best squaws. The High School girls were inclined to get a bit prissy. It was always the Central girls who squealed the loudest and kicked one up the backside the hardest.

Free-range hens enjoying life and youngsters joining in with the harvesting – a familiar childhood scene

Now, about this time, the farmer would usually have a stroll around. Did they want to chase the young varmints off? Indeed, no! They wanted to encourage the little perishers. Do you get the picture? The hay had to be turned over to get the sun well and truly on it. Now, it could be done by machine (which was hard work), or it could be done by dozens of yelling 'Indian Braves'. So, that's how the hay was well and truly done to a turn in those far-off days.

Ah! But the best was yet to come. No stinking lorries pulling into the field to pick up the hay in those days! No fear! Into the field clip-clopped our old faithful shire-horse again pulling a huge hay cart as it was called.

Ready with a full load of hay to return to the farm. The youngsters would all ride on top of the hay on the cart — a marvellous experience in the setting sun

'Now, come on you young rips', would yell out the farmer. 'Help load up hay – and it's ginger beer for all helpers. I said "ginger beer" young Davies – leave that cider alone! That's for my lads with pitch-forks.'

Oh, yes. Scrumpy was a great temptation in those brown earthenware bottles. But it was lethal. Even the grown-ups would roll home from loading up the hay carts singing at the top of their voices and landing in a ditch sometimes. They were a common lot (and I loved 'em all!).

But, of course, if any kids were slightly affected there would have been a lot of trouble. PC Jones would have had to investigate – my word!

So – it was ginger beer for us.

Kids and adults all used to gather the hay and load it on to the hay cart and take it in turns to pat Arthur the shire. He loved the attention from everybody. Vain old blighter he was. Well, he was the most important one there. He was the one to get the hay to the farm. Nobody else could.

The men with pitchforks could throw that stuff up high on that cart and it got bigger and bigger, until it was like a mobile haystack. (The cider helped, mind!) Oh, it was a jolly time for all.

Then came the big event! All up on top! Talk about riding top deck on a bus – nothing as exciting as riding on top of a load of hay.

How we got up on top, goodness knows. But we did. We used to dig our feet in the hay and make steps in it. It was a mad rush too. There was not room for everybody! Some would have to walk back. The shame of it.

The girls always got up first. They were better at it and, if any of their mates were left behind, they would just shove a dainty little foot into the face of a fierce young 'Indian brave' on the climb-up and he would land back on the field yelling blue murder!

When everybody who could get up there had got up, it was time to go. The farmer would shout out 'Off we go Arthur', and the magnificent shire would start the journey back to the farm, loaded up with at least two dozen squealing youngsters (as well as the huge load of hay).

There was a lorry in front of me the other day loaded up with those awful cubes and, as I sat behind its belching fumes in my car, I thought

'My goodness, this is progress'. As the lorry moved away I suddenly saw, in my mind's eye, the hay cart with bits of hay falling off down the lane and the trees with bits of hay stuck to their branches and the smell – the super hay smell as we sunk into it. No ride has ever thrilled me so much as those rides on the hay carts, with old Arthur clip-clopping along and the sun gradually sinking beyond the hills. Yes, the hay season in the 1930s cost nothing for us kids, but what entertainment it all was.

*Grandma and Grandpa
Taylor*

GRANDMA TAYLOR

'Your grandmother's coming to stay next week', my mother informed me. She had been reading a letter that had arrived in the morning post. My mother would always inform *me* when Grandma Taylor was coming to stay (not my father). She always said it loud enough so that PC 97 of the Gloucestershire Constabulary could hear, but the end result was the same as usual. 'Twas in the early 1930s and I looked up long enough from devouring the contents of the *Gem Weekly* (which had also arrived from the paper shop) to say 'All right Mum', before returning to the adventures of Tom Merry and Co. at St Jims.

My young brother didn't even bother to look up at all (being far too busy with Mrs Hippo and the Bruin Boys in his weekly *Playbox*). The cat, likewise, was unimpressed. On the other hand, our Airedale dog gazed soulfully at my mother and wandered outside to his kennel to consider this awful prospect.

PC 97 of the Gloucestershire Constabulary looked up from his *Daily Herald* and spoke. His comments amounted to two words, 'Must she?'

From the gentle little breakfast scene one could reckon that the visit of my mother's mother was not exactly an event to hang the flags out for.

Grandma Taylor was a solemn lady, who could never find any of the joys of life, unless you could count when she was singing her favourite hymn. I can't recall the title, but I do know that one line went, 'Lie me in the deep and narrow grave'.

She did smile at times and, I must confess, she was a tough old bird. Well, she used to listen in to the BBC on Sundays and enjoy it (and you had to be tough for that). Their idea of a light, jolly song in those days was 'Hark, Hark the Lark', sung by a boy soprano, whose name I don't remember.

She always enjoyed herself when she walked up from Rowanfield Road in Cheltenham to see her friend Maude, who lived in St George's Road. My grandparents lived in the big house by the railway crossing in those days, you see.

Grandma and Maude would take a bus ride every week to their favourite spot – the Cheltenham Cemetery. There, surrounded by graves and tombstones, they would sit and talk, then walk around to see where they would like to be buried one day. They really enjoyed that little outing. (Incidentally, my grandmother was laid to rest years later in her favourite weekly destination. She lived to the ripe old age of 80 before that though.)

The old folk took me to the cemetery once. I was not at all happy there. I got fed up just sitting, so I wandered around the gravestones.

One thing always puzzled me. I asked Grandma one day, 'Gran,' I said, 'where do they bury the wicked people? All I can find is people gone to heaven.' 'Don't be such a silly little boy', snapped Grandma (but she never did tell me).

The frigid relationship between Grandma and Father was due to the fact that Grandma always considered Mother had married beneath her.

Grandma didn't like policemen. She found them rather 'coarse'. As for alcohol in any shape or form – that was the devil's brew. No man who drank had a right to belong to the human race.

So, when Mother married a policeman who sank many a jar whenever the occasion arose (and it did often on the 10 p.m. to 6 a.m. shift), that was really going down the social scale. (In fact, it was way off it altogether.)

'He's common, well his whole family's common. Look at his mother. She's only got to open her mouth! Then that stupid Uncle Sid of his – the one who drives a tram and married that awful fat woman in the fish and chip shop! I've only met her once and she smelled all fish.'

I used to listen in rapt attention to it all. I had my own opinion about the whole thing. I was definitely on the side of the 'common'.

Fancy driving one of those great big grinding trams. Coo! That was better than going to the cemetery! Round by St James Railway Station in Cheltenham, making that lovely grinding sound on the curves. Ringing the bell at some poor old cyclist with his wheel caught in a rail. And working in a fish and chip shop! Actually working in one! You could take a chip any time.

As for my 'common' Grannie Jones (not Grandma, if you please), she was everybody's idea of the perfect grannie. She was big, round and jolly, with a face like a well-polished plate, and wore a pair of gold-plated spectacles that always slid down her nose.

She called my mother 'Lil', which used to send Mother into a simmering rage. 'I shan't go there any more', she used to say to Father after each visit. 'My name's Lilian. She makes me feel like some cheap thing from a music hall show.'

But Grannie Jones was my favourite one all right. The main reason was her homemade ice-cream. It was always in a tall tub in the corner of the front room, next to the aspidistra.

My young brother and I used to stand beside it, frightened it was all a dream and would have disappeared. Then, in would come Grannie Jones with two cups and fill them to the brim for us. To this day, I have never tasted such super ice-cream. All rich and yellow it was, nothing like the stuff you get today.

But, I must return to that fateful sentence, 'Your grandmother's coming to stay next week'. Alas, the wrong grandmother.

I went out and joined the Airedale in his kennel. He looked as if he had forgotten where he had buried his favourite bone! 'Cheer up, Bruce', I said. 'Let's go and round up the gang and get some tiddlers up in Old Dare's Pond. You can roll in the mud and get nice and wet.'

The Airedale lost his look of gloom. Off we went. Next week was a long way away.

GRANDPA TAYLOR AND THE WIRELESS

My most vivid memory of Grandpa Taylor was his arrival one day at our home with the wireless set under both arms. Yes, I did say 'both arms'. It was around 1932 and the new wonder of the age was really getting going. Everybody was buying wireless sets. What a load of equipment one set was too. (It's unbelievable when one looks at today's small, compact sets.)

Under one arm was the loudspeaker – a massive thing shaped like a swan's neck, with terminals on the base, and the other end like an ice-cream cone! The big box under Grandpa's other arm was the receiver. In his left hand he was carrying the low-tension Exide accumulator – a glass container, about 6 inches by 4 inches, filled with acid with plates in (like in a car battery). And, finally, in a bag, he had in his right hand the high-tension dry battery (a huge thing about as big as a large tissue box – double size).

How 'Old Gramp' got that lot down from the station, I'll never know. He'd bought the batteries at the local radio–record–gramophone–cycle shop (Mr Lovell's), which was a favourite haunt of us youngsters. There were lovely records to look at – Jack Payne, Jack Hylton, Ray Noble – with the famous little white dog on the label. Then there were the glistening new bikes to try out.

Mr Lovell was a jolly gent and he never minded us hanging around. In any case, his son Bernard was about our age, and he used to show us how all the new wireless sets worked and what the batteries were for. Very brainy was young Bernard. (We little knew that years later he would become Sir Bernard Lovell, England's leading astronomer.)

But, let's get back to the arrival of Grandpa and the great 'wonder of the age'.

Most gardens all over Britain in those days had long poles, as high as a house, stuck in the ground, with a wire attached and the other end fixed to the house. The poles were at the bottoms of the gardens. You never saw such a maze of poles. Talk about the Forest of Dean. You couldn't see along people's gardens for wireless poles. It's a wonder there was a tree left in the country!

Then, there were all the washing lines as well. Not many telephone wires though. People couldn't afford telephones in those days. (And with a super postal service costing just $1\frac{1}{2}$d. going out as late as 8 p.m. from the local box and delivered before 8 a.m. anywhere in the kingdom the next morning, who wanted phones?)

The wireless cables made a marvellous perch for the birds. Hundreds of them just sat on all the wires all day long. It was the normal sight!

So, of course, along with the rest, we had to have a tall pole erected in the garden. But that wasn't all. Oh, dear me, no!

Grandpa Taylor out shopping in the early 1930s. More wireless components?

Grandpa had come to start work. Now, Grandpa was an electrician on the LMS Railway and electricians in the early days of installation loved to bore holes in everything. He was no exception. Mother began to look very uneasy, as the hole boring began in the window-frame, through the door jamb and into the back of the sideboard. (He ruined many of Grandma's best sideboards with his holes. Like a woodpecker he was, once he got a brace and bit in his hand.)

There were wires everywhere. Outside now. A piece of pipe about 3 feet long belted into the flower bed outside the window. 'Father – whatever are you doing?', squealed my poor mum. 'You're ruining my daffodils and tulips.' Grandpa gave her a pitying look, as a great scientist would give a tea lady. 'The earth pipe, woman', he sighed. 'You can't have reception without earth wire.'

By this time, Alec from next door and Clifford over the road had joined me to watch this great construction work. This was better than dirt-tracking over the old tramroad.

Bruce, the intelligent Airedale, had bolted into his box by now and Smut, our cat, had gone to inform his mates over by the fish and chip shop that a mog can't get peace even in his own home these days.

So, the earth wire was duly fixed! Perhaps – maybe – sound! Aerial wire in – earth wire out. Not on your life!

Lightning arrester. Now, a switch had to be fixed in the window-sill to cut the aerial should there be a thunderstorm. 'Stops the lightning leaping out of the loudspeaker', explained Grandpa.

If a bomb was being planted in the room, there would not have been more fear in my mother's face by now. Even Father was beginning to look a little uneasy!

Only the 'fearless three' 11 year olds were enjoying every minute.

So, finally, with battery and accumulator in position, Grandpa started to twiddle the knobs. Can you imagine the space taken up by all this contraption? It was unbelievable! Everybody stood well back!

Suddenly the room filled with music and everybody applauded. Grandpa had won!

Alec, Clifford and I stood with mouths open in ecstasy. It was Jack Payne and his Orchestra. Yes, so it was! 'No more buying records for these youngsters now', beamed Father. Payne was really big in the early 1930s, you see. No pop group today can touch that big dance band for popularity. He was on every day and nearly every evening. He was a household name with Grandmas and 6 year olds alike. All the music in those days was listened to by young and old alike, and everybody knew the words and (what was more) everybody sang the songs at work, in the street, at home – everywhere!

So, that's how the wireless arrived at our home. It was the start of a complete new life for us youngsters.

With Radio Luxembourg starting up in 1933 and driving the BBC mad (because they took all their young listeners), we quite forgot our tiddlers, hay carts and Indian raids.

'We are the Ovalteenies, little girls and boys.' Yes, we all wore our Ovalteeny badges and listened in regularly to that top Luxembourg show. Then there was the Horlicks Picture House Hour, Zambuk Ointment, Owbridges Lung Tonic, Macleans Stomach Powder and Bile Beans. A day listening to Luxembourg in those days gave one the impression it was run by a huge chemist's Shop.

It's not much fun these days, just turning on a switch. How much more exciting it was to have poles and wires, glass batteries and lightning arresters.

On wild, windy nights these days the radio doesn't suddenly go dead and a torch light reveal in the dark a wireless pole crashed down over the neighbour's chicken house. No, it's just a bore in glorious VHF. And it's also very noticeable as well that the reception is nowhere near as good these days as it was in the Golden Days of wireless.

'NORTHFIELD', ROWANFIELD ROAD

A visit to my grandparents' home was always an event for me when I was in my pre-teen years, way back in the early 1930s. They lived in the big house by the Alstone Railway Crossing in Cheltenham and, my word, what a place for a young lad like me to play in.

There was a big, gloomy cellar, lit by a single electric lamp and a huge pile of coal in one corner. This coal was shot down through a trapdoor from outside, by the coalman, once a year (perhaps 2 or 3 tons at a time) and that would last right through the winter. Now, cellars in those days were known as 'coal cellars' and that was why.

A huge slice of bacon would be hanging in another corner, on a massive hook, and that would last for months. Also, a big meat safe would contain all sorts of cheese, fruit and leftovers. It was, in fact, the refrigerator of the olden days and, because the cellar kept so cool all the time, the food was perfectly fresh.

The house had big rambling rooms up and down, and outhouses and sheds galore. Also, much to my great delight, at the bottom of the garden were ten well-contented white, brown and black chickens. (We called them fowls, not chickens.) I used to feed them that super Indian corn.

My greatest delight was in the autumn when the plums were ripe. Victoria plums and those beautiful, big, yellow plums. By the age of 8 I was a good tree climber and, by the age of 11, an expert. I used to shin up the trees and gorge plums between meals, and then Mother and Grandmother would wonder why I had 'the runs' after scoffing down a huge helping of plum tart and custard at dinner time as well!

Of course, just sitting up in a tree would soon become boring, so I used to improve the shinning hour (as it were) by bestowing my attention on next door, where there was a village school. When the youngsters came out

The marvellous tree-lined promenade in Cheltenham in the 1930s — Grandma's favourite walk

to play, I would pelt them with overripe plums and make derogatory remarks at those 'common old Cheltenham kids with holes in their trousers'. I was a dreadful snob then because Grandma and Grandpa lived in this great house.

I got away with that for a while, until one day when I ambled around to the local sweetshop and got ambushed. A 'hit squad' were waiting for me and I was well and truly belted by great clods of earth, until I looked like something from the local allotments. I decided from then on just to eat those plums.

There was a huge elderberry tree on the front lawn and Grandpa used to make some super elderberry wine down in the cellar. He used to sample it too, down there. He was a great singer, was my Grandpa, but he would always sing hymns. So, as soon as we heard 'Abide with Me' coming up from the cellar, we knew the year's wine was a great success.

When my uncle used to visit and my dad as well, and all three got down there, it was more likely to be 'If you Were the Only Girl in the World and I Was the Only Boy', mind you!

Of course, all these goings on were on weekdays. Now, Sundays were not so good! Grandma would have nothing done on a Sunday. No tree climbing and no playing trains up and down the garden path. It's a wonder the poor old fowls got fed. The only work allowed was getting meals. Once Dad started to do a bit of digging up by the toolshed and the row went on for hours after. So, Sundays were a bit of a trial.

To make matters worse, Grandpa actually had an organ in the front room, and he used to open the window in the summer and play to Miss Roberts, their lodger in the room above. She used to open her window as well. 'Oh, Mr Taylor, you do play so beautifully', she used to say to him. (He used to like her to praise him.) So next time we would get a song as well. (The rest of the family used to shut themselves away in a far room.) I had to suffer, however, packed out of 'harm's way' with Grandpa.

Now, 'The Holy City' is a beautiful song, but when Grandfather used to sing it loudly and blast away at that organ, I used to wish it had never been written. Also, that room didn't help. Long velvet curtains hung from the big, tall windows and there was a huge picture that covered the whole

Grandma Taylor and me during one of my stays at her home in Cheltenham in the late 1920s

length of the room on one side of some shepherd or other having a dream and lots of funny little boys floating around in the air blowing trumpets above him. I suppose that was art, but my idea of art in those days was *Tiger Times Weekly*, *Mrs Hippo's Annual*, and Laurel and Hardy films.

Miss Roberts was a poor, middle-aged lady, highly educated, who just kept to her room all the time. She even had her meals there. My brother and I were scared out of our life when she used to creep out for her walk around the lawn. It was my cousin's fault. He came down from Birmingham one weekend and brought his *Grimm's Fairy Tales* book with him, which was full of witches and goblins and things that go bump in the night.

After taking a look at Miss Roberts, he told us she was definitely a witch, since he had read about somebody like her in his book. Well, she looked so queer. (Actually she was cast out from a rich family, disowned because she had an illegitimate child when she was young and Grandma was sworn to secrecy. Poor soul – it was very sad. But I learned this years later.)

She used to suck white peppermints, but, when she approached us to give us one, we would bolt upstairs. That cousin had told us that if we had her peppermints, we would turn into frogs and I didn't fancy living around the rhubarb patch for the rest of my life.

It's hard to believe now that the sprawling housing estate, named Hesters Way, was just beautiful big fields stretching to Alstone Lane in the 1930s, but it was.

Alstone Lane was just that. It was a lane, dusty in the summer, muddy in the winter, full of potholes, where the only traffic would be an occasional horse and cart. On fine Sunday evenings Grandma used to take little Terry for a walk through the fields to see the cows and sheep, clamber over stiles and meander alongside the brook.

Across the meadows, I remember, we used to hear the sound of church bells and around us, the twitter of many birds, large and small.

The air was fresh and clean and, when I got back to Grandma's home, my shoes were covered with the yellow powder from thousands of buttercups.

This was quite different from the petrol-laden fumes we breathe in around Hesters Way today. Such is progress. The beautiful Cheltenham of my childhood days, alas, is no more.

Beer Bottles and Tar Barrells
at Cashes Green

BEER BOTTLES

Cashes Green, near Stroud, in the 1930s, was surrounded by large fields to play in, muddy streams to fall in and huge trees where the junior Tarzans swung from ropes and fell off branches, and must have started the Elastoplast manufacturers on their way to a fortune.

I was one of those great adventurers at the age of 12, so really I should have had no worries in the world.

But I did and so did the rest of the swinging Tarzans. There were times when we had to go without our liquorice sherbert fountains, often because we just didn't have the halfpenny.

In those days it was a maximum of sixpence a week and that was subject to deductions for ripped trousers, smashed windows and squirting Old Ma Brown with water pistols. 'I'll tell your Mother', she said and she did too.

It was Cranham Feast that put us on the way to wealth. In two words – beer bottles. You see, the revellers at the Feast every year would buy dozens of bottles of beer from the Royal William and cart them into the 'bush' (as it were), there to consume the same. But they would just leave them lying in the grass afterwards and that was that.

Now, we young businessmen soon cottoned on to the idea of collecting the empties and returning them to the Royal William the next day. The landlord was only too happy to give us the penny deposit on each (and, my word, there was tuppence on a quart cider bottle – a real bonus).

With dozens of bottles in cardboard boxes handed in, we were in the upper income bracket. We could collect up to about 3 shillings each, depending on how many of us were around at the time.

My mother at our Cashes Green home in the late 1930s

It was a week of joy and goodwill after. Harry Collins even bought little Janet Gardiner a 2-ounce bar of Cadbury's milk chocolate out of the proceeds. (Mind you, the rest of us didn't approve of such wild extravagance. Those Cadbury Milks were tuppence each).

Sherbert fountains should have been enough for her. He could never get Janet to bite on a sherbert fountain liquorice after that. She was a 'Milk Tray woman' for ever after.

I was able to buy a *Sexton Blake Library*, as well as a *Gem, Magnet, Hotspur* and *Wizard* that week.

Then the whole gang of us could clear off to the Gaumont in Stroud to thrill to *Hopalong Cassidy*, or Jimmy Cagney's *G Men* (only sixpence before 3.30 p.m. if it was a 'U' certificate).

But, what were we to do when the filthy lucre ran out? Oh, youth in the mid-1930s were very quick off the mark when the cash ran low. What about calling around the houses for empty bottles? Willy Smith had a super box-truck (with the best pram wheels he could find over the tip).

The idea caught on. People couldn't be bothered to take their beer bottles back to the pub. 'We'll take your old beer bottles away for you for nothing, Mrs Davis.' 'How kind of you, my little man. They're just round the back!' Soon the truck filled up.

Mind you, we were too clever to take them back to one pub. Oh no – three here, four there, two somewhere else. The publicans always shelled out. They never knew we were touring the district for bottles.

Now, we could have carried on like that quite successfully if Lanky Harris hadn't been nosing around Stroud Brewery's bottle tip one day. 'There's a dozen of 'em', he yelped, 'not broken! We can just get 'em from there instead of ploughing round the houses.'

You see, someone wasn't doing their job properly. Only broken bottles were supposed to be on the tip, but somebody was dumping dirty bottles as well (labels quite all right). All that was needed was to wash 'em. Norman was chosen as washer agent 'cause his mum was a widow and went out to work all day. There were no nosy mothers around his house to want to know where all the bottles were coming from.

So the great business flourished. We collected bottles from the brewery dump and took them to the Stroud Brewery pubs, who paid us our pennies and who then claimed the pennies back from the Stroud Brewery. (I suppose, in time, the same bottles would land back on the dump and start their cycle again. It was a great business.)

Mind you, we did have a pang of conscience at times, but quickly reckoned out that nobody was losing any money. It just went round and round with the bottles, so everybody was happy.

But all good things come to an end. Why old 'Bobby' Green had to be patrolling around by the dump one day, goodness knows. But he was. 'Clear off you young devils', he bellowed, 'or I'll cuff the lot of you around the ears.' (He would have too. There was instant punishment those days from the officers of the law.) We all got too scared after.

Harry Collins found another girlfriend who was content with sherbert fountains. As far as the rest of us? Well, the conker season was about to begin. We had other things of great importance to concentrate on. Mind you, I often wonder if Stroud Brewery questioned why the empty bottles didn't come in so often all of a sudden!

TAR BARRELS AND STEAMROLLERS

It was Wacko Brown who brought the good news. He rushed down to the tiddler pond on his bike and was so excited he forgot the brakes didn't work, and landed bike and all, right where the best tiddlers were swimming. We all let out howls of protest, because we had been doing pretty well up till then getting the little fish nicely captured in our jam jars.

Wacko had sent them all away. We didn't have the courtesy to help him retrieve both his bike and himself, so we got the bike out of the water!

But Wacko didn't seem to mind wet trousers and muddy knees that particular very hot August morning. He had great news to tell us. 'The barrels are being dropped', he gasped, 'all over North Road and West, and up by the school and down by the pub.'

Gosh, we were all ears at once. We knew what that meant. Tar spraying was going to start. The big tank on wheels with the roaring fire box underneath, and all that lovely hot bubbling tar and the piles of grit left by the council horse and cart. It was marvellous stuff to play in and put bits down the back of those tough little girls' dresses (when they weren't looking).

And – the steamroller. The main event. That huge rumbling, hissing monster that rolled the grit into the tar. We almost worshipped the steamroller.

Next to becoming a driver on the loco of the Pines Express down to Bournemouth, this was it. To drive a steamroller.

So, Wacko was indeed 'the bearer of good tidings' that fine morning. Here was salvation at last. An end to boredom. You see, all the hay had been safely gathered in and the apples weren't yet ripe enough for 'scrogging' around the local orchards. Cricket should have been in full swing down at the 'Rec', but it had to be temporarily suspended, due to the fact that Old Man Baker had threatened us all with a sound walloping if we came

*My father at our Cashes Green
home in the late 1930s*

within 200 yards of his house, which happened to front on to the field.

It really was Willy Howard's fault. He was a great batsman and was forever scoring sixes. Unfortunately, Old Man Baker's missus was sitting sunning herself one morning by her front door (with the door open to let in some air), when Willy belted one straight past her head and straight through the front door and halfway up the stairs with a terrific bang. She let out a yelp like a fire engine siren, and Old Baker kept our ball and threatened us with violence.

We bought a new ball and peace was restored, as we all warned Willy to stop slogging them so hard. Would you believe it? Little Eric Smith (who usually hit a couple, then was bowled out) suddenly belted a loose ball high up in the air. Then there was a dreadful crash of broken glass. It went straight through Baker's front window and just missed the old cat asleep there. Old Baker hurtled out of his gate, nearly tripping over an hysterical 'moggie' and the missus did another 'fire siren'.

63

We all belted off in all directions, which was why the Cashes Green Test Series with Stonehouse had been suspended and why we were bored, and why the good tidings of tar barrels was so welcome.

Next Monday morning the pungent smell of the tar was a signal for almost the whole junior population to turn out to watch and wonder. But there were also several mothers wheeling their ailing infants to the scene (those who happened to have a bad chest or whooping cough). This was so they could inhale the tar fumes, which were reckoned to be a sure-fire cure for chest ailments. Certainly it did help the young ones. Come to think of it, many chest lozenges, even today, contain creosote, which was the same thing, so they weren't as mad as it may seem.

The boiling tar was siphoned to metal pipes held by two men with leather pads strapped to their hands, wearing corduroy trousers tied with string below the knee and huge black boots. At the end of the pipes were nozzles that sprayed the tar in a good, thick, even layer all over the road. This was a highly skilled job, because every bit of road had to be covered.

Then came two more men who would shovel up piles of sand and gravel, and (with uncanny skill) spread it all over the lake of tar, so evenly that it was a job to see much tar when they had done. Then off they went steadily up the road, followed by mothers pushing prams and all of us kids watching them go. They did one side of the road at a time, of course, so as not to hold up the traffic for long.

But, of course, we held back because there was a rumbling and a squeak-ing, and the whole road seemed to shudder as the star attraction arrived – the huge steamroller hissing steam and dozens of things all moving and groaning at the same time. They were very similar to the ones you see at the steam fairs now, with the addition of a huge concrete roller on the front.

That great steamroller would leave the road with a beautiful, tightly packed surface, with only a very few loose bits of grit in the gutter and no sweeping up after into great piles like they do nowadays. (What a contrast to the appalling way they leave the roads today, with loose stones flying about everywhere when you drive over them.)

So that particular week passed very well for all of us lads. When the great monster was rolled on to the side of the road for the night and the fire raked out, most of us managed to persuade the driver to let us get up with him and twiddle the controls. Now, I ask you, what could be a greater thrill than to be up there in charge of a steamroller, even if it wasn't moving!

But, after the feast, as always, the reckoning!

Without doubt the busiest shopkeeper in the district the next day was the chemist. Also the happiest!

You just can't get up on oily steamrollers, clamber up over tar barrels, dive into heaps of grit and sand, and come home looking as if you have just left school. We had to face the wrath of our despairing mothers with a job to do.

The chemist? Ah! He knew his juniors, he did! He was well stocked up with tar remover, wasn't he? Yes, there weren't many mums who didn't visit him the next day. Shoes, socks and trousers, not to mention knees and arms were all dabbed and dabbed with Mr Turner's tar remover.

It was no use telling us we must not go near the tar spraying. That was like telling us not to go down by the bridge and watch the 'Cheltenham Flyer' go by every afternoon! What a man's gotta do, he's gotta do!

Down by the tiddler pond a few days later, all was quiet when Wacko Brown arrived on the scene again. He didn't ride into the tiddlers this time. He had actually had his brakes seen to and stopped so suddenly he went over the handlebars and nosedived into the buttercups. 'Well?' we demanded. 'They're coming,' he gasped. 'The posters are up on the fish shop wall.' We knew what he meant! The fair, of course, with tons of noise and lots of music and – gosh – more big traction engines!

Was there no end to the social whirl of 12 year olds?

GINGER BEER AND HORSES

We always knew when Pickups Ginger Beer truck had arrived at Cashes Green during the school holidays, because it was just around the same time that Norman Nicholls's mother called him for dinner. In those far-off days in the 1930s the pop wagons and ice-cream vans didn't have bells and chimes to announce their presence as they do today. So Pickups Ginger Beer had a good free 'Here we are'.

Now, if all this seems rather confusing, let me try to clarify the picture.

You see, Norman's ma had a voice that (should air raids have been a regular thing over Stroud) would have stood in for any air-raid siren. She started on a low note and went up to such great, great heights that every moggie within a quarter of a mile scampered for cover and all the birds that sat on the telephone wires outside her house took off as one! (Never to be seen again for a good hour.)

So, the beginning of Norman started with a low 'Nor' – and finished at – 'man', so high and screeching that I just could not hope to imitate it.

At the sound of that ear-shattering screech, Norman, who was about 10 years old, would drop everything (even his precious tiddlers at times) and bolt up the road to his home.

The rest of us would follow at a more leisurely speed in anticipation of the sight of Pickups Ginger Beer truck, plus the entertainment.

Norman's ma would always be standing out by the front gate and was ready to deliver a blow across Norman's right ear as he rushed past her in for his dinner. This was because Norman should have been at home for dinner and not making the good lady have to call him in (like he was No. 27 on the boating lake).

Sometimes Norman caught it, a right hefty wallop. But sometimes he dodged it by skilful ducking under the heavy hand. Thus the entertainment. Billy Russell ran a book on the event. Five-to-one in fag cards whether Norman would catch a wallop or not. The betting was heavy. If Norman dodged his wallop we all got five cards for our one. But, if old Ma Nicholls won, then the 'Ladbrokes' collected.

This breathtaking event every Tuesday was followed by gathering around Pickups pop man and, having made sure he had plenty of 'fizz and belch' aboard, clearing off to our homes to get out last week's empty and ask our mothers for the necessary sixpence.

Now, notice that I said 'empty', not 'empties'. The ginger beer was delivered in large, heavy earthenware jars, with a screw top made of the same material. One was enough for the week for a family of four, believe me. And the thick jar kept the drink lovely and cool.

Pickups was a Bristol firm and today their jars are collectors' items. The Second World War stopped a lot of their business and I can't remember seeing them after. Of course, Corona came in as well in the 1930s and lasted well into the present day. (A little more expensive now than back in my childhood days though.) A box of four was delivered to your home for tenpence (and that was fivepence on the wooden box – returnable). So, four large bottles of Corona pop cost fivepence before the War. (That was a shilling.) Many people just had two bottles for sixpence (which would be $2^{1}/_{2}$p today.)

By the end of the 1930s traders had vans and horses. Those marvellous animals hadn't faded out by any means. The Cainscross Co-op used to deliver their bread in green vans pulled by an intelligent 'gee-gee' around our way. It was a fascinating sight.

Along the road would come the horse and van, with the driver looking very smart in cap and uniform, with 'Co-op' on both items. He would never say a word to old Ben the horse. Ben would stop at every house where the Co-op dropped bread. It was uncanny. He would slowly walk past maybe four or five houses, then stop at one, then on he would go again, then stop again. Maybe a group of half a dozen houses would come up. Ben would stop at every one. Never a mistake.

He knew which road to go into next as well. All the roundsman had to do was take down a big basket, fill it with loaves and cakes, down the garden path and back, put the basket back on the van and say 'Gee-up' and off they would go to the next customer.

Now, you couldn't get a van today to go along on its own, could you? Stopping at the right house every time.

Not only that. Ben was the best horse around for manure. Oh, yes, it was the thing to get out our little wooden trucks and shovels and follow the tradesmen's horses. The girls did it as well. It was the finest stuff out for roses and strawberries. So, as soon as 'Ben-the-Co-op' showed up, we followed him like birds after a plough.

As soon as the gentle giant did the necessary, rivals were at the ready waiting for the van to move on. Then, as soon as the coast was clear, in rushed the work parties and the first to the pile won. The disappointed losers would rush on after the Co-op awaiting the next time Ben rewarded the road with rose manure.

The animal must often have wondered why he was so popular. The kids fed him sugar and all sorts of vegetables all the time – hopefully!

But it really was quite a business. Little boys and girls (if their fathers didn't have a garden) came knocking on doors. 'Want some manure, Mrs Hopkins? Fresh Co-op best.' 'Oh, all right. Tip it over there.' 'Sixpence please, Mrs Hopkins'. 'All right, here you are.'

The best story I've ever heard about intelligent horses was told to me by my father. This was a regular thing in Cheltenham in the early 1920s when Dad used to live there before I was born.

There was a rag and bone man who used to turn up to his local in the Lower High Street every Saturday on his trap with his little pony in the shafts. Now, Old Herbert could sink one jar and then sink about a dozen more. Beer was threepence a pint then. So it was that he was out flat at closing time. But the lads knew what to do.

Every Saturday night they would carry him out to his pony and trap and put him on the trap fast asleep. Then they would say to the pony, 'Home boy' and off would go the strange combination clip-clopping down the road. About half a mile they would go, right to Herbert's home. Without fail. Herbert's wife and son would lift him off the trap and put him to sleep it off on the sofa.

The pony was rewarded with his oats and put to bed. The pantomime would be repeated again next Saturday.

There's nothing I would love more than to see the Co-op horse pull up outside my gate again, believe me, but sadly those days are with us no more.

APPLES WITH ROSIE

Not many people haven't heard about Laurie Lee's famous novel *Cider with Rosie*, in which the action takes place in the village of Slad near Stroud.

On the other hand, not many people have heard about 'Apples with Rosie', in which the action takes place in a small village near Stonehouse.

I shall now delve into the deep and dusky past of the 1930s and unfold this great epic.

Rosie went to Central School in Stroud and lived in this small village near Stonehouse. She was 14 years old and, without doubt, extremely popular with Marling and Central boys. She was most unpopular with High School girls, because she was so popular with Marling School boys.

You see, High School and Marling were the 'uppercrust' so to speak and High School girls expected Marling School to give their attention to their

Taking in the sun at Stratford Park Lido, around 1938, with two pals from Central & Marling School. I'm the good looking one! Notice the old box camera on the wall

equals on the social scale. Or, to put it more plainly, 'You don't mix with girls whose fathers take the *Daily Mirror*, when, with a little extra effort, tie straight and shoes given the old 'Cherry Blossom' now and then, you can speak to High School young ladies whose fathers take the *Daily Telegraph*.'

So, now why was 'Central School Rosie' the centre of attention? Why were there little groups of young gentlemen always chatting up Rosie around September, whilst leaning on their Dawes, Raleighs and Hercules cycles? Why did Rosie always have plentiful supplies of Cadbury's milk or Cadbury's plain and always seemed to be sucking a Walls ice-cream, yet never stopping the man 'and buy one'? (As his invitation demanded on his dark blue tricycle.)

Certainly, it was *not* because Rosie bestowed her favours (to put it discreetly). Rosie, in fact, was very naïve. She thought sex was what they delivered coal in!

No, in one word, it was *apples*.

You see, Rosie knew every apple orchard around her district and, what was more to the point, Rosie knew the comings and goings of the owners of the apple orchards. She knew when Old Johnson took his missus to the local whist-drive for a couple of hours and when Charlie Price was off to the Stroud Gaumont with his missus. She knew when other owners were down the local and when they were not. In other words, Rosie knew when the coast was clear!

So, the custom was for some of us worthy examples of 'Marling School gentry' to meet Rosie and all cycle away to her chosen 'Apple of the Night' orchard. Without the young lady there would have been problems. Having safely gathered in the apples the big question was where to put them to get them safely home to our various hideaways where our parents wouldn't find them.

We had to be very careful in our Marling School uniform, you see. It wasn't a case of just cycling off in our old 'knock-about' clothes. Suspicious parents would ask 'Why haven't you got your blazer on and where's your cap?' So we had to go apple scrogging in our school uniforms, which meant no zippers with big pockets for apples galore.

Rosie was our apple carrier, as well as our country scout. You see, in the 1930s, schoolgirls didn't wear shirts inside their skirts as they do today.

Stratford Park Lido in the 1930s, when we had to queue to get in on a hot day

They all had blouses with elastic around the waist, outside their skirts. Excellent for carrying apples in.

So, into the chosen orchard we would go, shin up the trees, pick the fruit and lob them down to Rosie, who would drop them into her blouse, where the elastic waist would hold them very nicely out of sight. That girl should have been in our first eleven cricket team, for she caught apple after apple without hardly ever dropping one.

When she announced that the blouse held an 'elastic bursting load', down the trees we would clamber and, keeping a weather eye open for 'all clear', innocently mount our cycles and glide away into the evening sun, leaving our 'little girl' to go her own sweet way on her cycle (apart from us, of course).

71

Later we would all meet safely up some lane and Rosie would produce the apples out of her neckline like a conjuror producing white rabbits, and into our different saddlebags they would all go.

She wasn't all that keen on apples, but she was keen on Cadbury's milk or Cadbury's plain, which we had to supply her with. They cost tuppence each, mind you, but we reckoned it was fair enough exchange!

This little arrangement kept us well supplied with apples for many weeks and, of course, thanks to Rosie, nobody ever noticed a few apples missing. With a few taken from many orchards, the effort was a winner. One month, Form 4B seemed to live on apples!

Mind you, Rosie did confess that she raised a few eyebrows one day when she went into the post office. Buxom schoolgirls were not unknown, but a blouse full of 6 pounds of Cox's Orange Pippins absolutely startled the customers!

But one bright evening we were busy as usual up a nice big apple tree dropping fruit down to Rosie, and I happened to shout down, 'Got a blouse full yet, Rosie?' and a deep harsh voice bellowed back. 'My name's not Rosie, you young villain, and I've got a good thick stick here ready to greet you when you've kindly finished.'

It was Old Johnson fairly bristling with rage. Not Rosie. (We found out later she had seen Old Johnson coming and had bolted before he saw her.) We slid down the tree and bolted, but not before a few whacks got us across the backside, plus a painful interview with our headmaster later.

It was the end of our particular contract with Rosie. 'I shall never get married', moaned Lanky Lane. 'You just can't trust a woman! Want a piece of Cadbury's plain?'

FIREWORKS

Fireworks week was always the big one for all us gangsters, engine drivers, outlaws, cowboys and G Men in our village in the 1930s. Gangsters, engine drivers, outlaws, cowboys and G Men all went on leave in order to gather together in preparation for the Great Day – 5 November, Bonfire Night.

But activities started a good week ahead. The hills were alive with the sound of bangs and more bangs (definitely not music).

Old ladies were complaining down at the Police Station about jumping jacks leaping behind them when they came out of the post office after collecting their pensions. Unpopular old gentlemen complained about sudden bangs occurring behind them as they cycled along to the local.

These bangs were the end result of a brilliant piece of workmanship thought up by Lanky Harris. A piece of string was tied on to the unsuspecting victim's bicycle rear mudguard (about 3 yards long) when he was in one of the shops. On the end of the string was fastened on the Standard Fireworks Little Demons (at half a penny each they were the real bargains, with an almighty bang that would make your shirt shoot up your back).

As soon as the 'marked man' mounted his cycle one of our gang would 'light the blue touch paper and retire'. In fact, all of us would retire – double quick. With Little Demon trailing behind on its string well alight, our gallant cyclist would pedal away for a few yards, then came the almighty bang, which made him quite excited! It went down all the better, because we always chose our subjects well and knew there would be a roar of curses calculated to turn the air the traditional 'blue'.

Watching from a safe distance, then gradually moving back, we were fascinated by the coversation of some of the shopping mothers. 'Never heard such language, Mrs Brown, disgusting I call it'. 'I should think so, Mrs Adams.' (A glance at the returning 'hit men'.) 'It's a good job these little boys weren't around to hear.'

The little boys assumed the required looks of perplexed choirboys. 'Hear what, Mrs Brown?' 'Never you mind, my little man. I suppose you've come to see what fireworks you're going to buy for Bonfire Night.' 'Oh yes, Mrs Brown, we're allowed to come and buy some tomorrow.' (I sometimes wonder at the innocence of adults way back then, I really do.)

We all got our fireworks in those days by joining the 'Firework Club'. Every shop had a firework club, which started in mid-summer. We each had a little card on which was recorded our weekly contribution – a penny.

Then, on 3 November, came the time when we could bring in our cards and 'cash in' as it were. By then parents and adult friends and relations had tipped us with sundry coins, so we usually had in the region of half a crown. And you could get an awful lot of fireworks for half a crown in the 1930s.

What a wonderful time we had making out lists of all our wants. Almost every shop stocked fireworks. Lovely great bundles of Little Demons, Big Demons, Little Wonders, Big Wonders, Martian Comets, Egyptian Palms, Speedway Sliders, rockets and the big, big one (priced fourpence), the Brock's Guy Fawkes Mine. What a crasher that one was.

Our folks gave us somewhat of a free hand. If we had our way we'd have had all Big Demons and Speedway Sliders. But we had to have some pretty ones as well, much to our disgust. 'Your Mother wants to see the Egyptian Palm and some rockets. She doesn't want to have her ears blasted by Big Demons all night.'

So we compromised. But we always kept back a few Little Demons in our pockets. There were dirty deeds to do around unpopular people, for which was needed a box of matches and a halfpenny Demon.

List completed, we would be down the shops, and back we would come and lay our treasures all out on the table. It seemed a shame to set them all off on Bonfire Night. They looked so attractive.

On 6 November we used to roam around looking for all the spent firework cartridges and we would collect them up and save them carefully for months after – get them out at times and relive the precious memories.

One Bonfire Night, though, didn't have such pleasant memories. You see, the best bang you could possibly get was a Big Demon in a dustbin. Especially if it was somebody's dustbin in the space between two houses. It was a risky business, but the end result was worth it.

The 'volunteer' had to creep along the garden path of the victim, carefully lift the lid of the dustbin, light the firework, drop it in the bin, quickly replace the lid and run like blue blazes. This particular night I was the 'volunteer' and I did the job well.

Off went the Demon with a tremendous roar, sending the lid up into the air and down again with a terrible crash. We were delighted until, 'You idiot', yelled my mate Ginger. 'You've put it in the wrong dustbin. Strewth, you've put it in old Bobby Green's bin.' (Our hated enemy lived next door.) Not much doubt about that. A door opened. A roar like a bull and out charged PC Green. My word, we ran half a mile before he gave up. It frightened the life out of us. (He had a heavy hand, did Old Green.)

A couple of days after my father said, 'Do you know anything about fireworks in dustbins the other night, my lad?' I wore my best look of surprise. 'Fireworks in dustbins, Dad? Coo, that's wasting them isn't it? No fear.'

HEIGH-HO! A SHOPPING WE WILL GO

Yes, it's back to the times of strange phrases like 'Made in England'. A look back to the times when there were shops. D'you remember shops?

They were places where assistants served you, smiled at you and asked if your back was better, or how the sprouts and peas were getting along up the allotments.

Now, I can remember going into shops and just calling out what my Mother had written on the grocery list, whilst a kindly lady brought everything to me and put it all in a nice little box, pushed it across a nice big counter and gave me fourpence change out of a £1 note.

That paid for the weekly groceries for the four of us. 'And I expect you'd like a sherbert fountain young man, wouldn't you?' That meant one of those marvellous Barrett's sherberts in a long yellow tube with a 4-inch stick of liquorice stuck out of it. Oh, the supreme ecstasy when, after five or six frantic sucks, the sherbert was up and into your mouth. Then the careful operation of tipping the last remains into your mouth without spilling it down the front of your new jersey. (Only experts like my particular gang could get that right, though there were times when some horrible little child would belt you on the back just at the crucial minute and the whole lot would shoot down your neck).

Of course, the sherbert fountains came free with big orders of nearly £1 a week.

But, by far the favourite shops for us youngsters around Stroud in the 1930s were the fish and chip shops. What bargains were to be had indeed! The usual order was a penny worth of chips. That was the same amount you have to pay 45p for today. (In '1930 money' that's 108 pence, quite an increase from one penny, I think you'll agree.)

When I lived in Bisley there used to be a travelling fish and chip van that arrived once a week. I can still picture it now in the gathering dusk of a winter's day, with a beautiful red glow from the coke fire and smoke pouring up from the tall chimney.

That super smell. Gosh – it was a mad rush to get there first.

'Evening, Mrs Brown. Four fish – that'll be eightpence and fourpenn'oth of chips. Shilling please, Mrs Brown.'

Can you credit it? Just 5p for a fish and chip tea for four! And enough for the cat as well! Yes, those cods were just very thinly coated with batter in those days. No sardines lost in a slab of batter like you get today. (Our cat used to get a bigger helping than one of the poor little things you get today.) We got a huge great piece of fish wrapped up in several sheets of good, reliable newspaper.

Oh yes! You could read all the news you may have missed. Have a good read whilst pawing away at the chips and groping into the lush white fish if you weren't going home. Your greasy little paws well wiped in the *Daily Mirror*, *Citizen* or *Daily Herald* after as well. You just don't get refined packages like that these days, now do you?

Later at Cainscross we had an even better deal. Wait until closing time, then dive in! 'Can we have the scrumpies please?' The scrumpies were the small bits of chips left over in the frying pan. It was unheard of in those days to include them in your chips like they do now.

Fancy! The cheery red-faced owner and his assistant used to ladle out a huge helping of scrumpies to about a half a dozen little hungry boys in a lovely big bag and all for free.

In return we used to bring in all the week's newspapers. All the fish and chip shops used to rely on the public's support with newspapers. Actually, they were excellent for keeping the contents very hot and the grease in as well.

So, what happened to the little red order books? In remote parts of the district all the grocers used to deliver as a matter of course. Mum had two order books. She would write down all her grocery needs in one and the van would collect it to start – then, when the groceries arrived with the book, Mum would pay the bill and hand the driver the second order book for next week. So it went on. It was a marvellous system. They even did it in the town too if you wanted them to.

It was a wonderful service if you were ill. There was never any worry about supplies. Civilization hadn't arrived. The horrors of the age had yet to come! There was not a supermarket in sight for many a year.

When I came into Gloucester with Mother to shop in the big places, I was always fascinated by the Maypole shop in Eastgate Street. All the assistants wore long, white aprons, and talked and smiled. But they were showmen as well. The Maypole specialized in butter and the big act was when the assistant got going with his butter-patting. It was like being at the seaside. I used to stand and watch in utter amazement.

From great piles of butter in the window he would mould rabbits and cows, and all sorts of pretty things (just like making things out of sand). The window was just filled with butter in all forms of things. People would just stand and watch. The assistants used to preen themselves like film stars. Well, it *was* very clever. I confided to my pal Willy, 'I'm going to be a butter-basher at the Maypole when I leave school.' Gosh, what a job! All those girls gazing at you in admiration!

'Where do you work, Terry?' 'At the Maypole' – pause – 'I make butter rabbits for the window display'. Looks of admiration from the High School and Central. Yes, it was going to be the Maypole for me when I left school.

Then on to tea at the Cadena in Eastgate Street. Or a mug of tea and a bun at Joe Lyons on the Cross and a 'Selection from the Desert Song' at Boots Café (opposite the Bon Marche) from the Palm Court Trio thrown in for free with your morning coffee!

All gone now – and Gloucester is a much sadder place without them.

'Be Prepared' — A Tale of Scouting Activities

'I'm going to join the Stonehouse Scouts', I announced to my mother and father one bright spring morning. The year was 1938 and we lived in Cashes Green, near Stroud.

'How nice', said my Mother. 'After all, you did quite well as a little Wolf Cub at Bisley, didn't you?' This was because, when we moved from Bisley to Cashes Green in 1935, I had two metal stars pressed into my Cub cap. A two-star Cub was a 'top-drawer Cub', you see.

How I got awarded it I'll never know. I think it was because I did less damage than most of the other wild Cubs of Bisley. Or probably because I used to devote some time 'off duty' going around to the Cub master's mother and asking her if she would teach me to play croquet properly on her lawn. (They call this 'greasing'.)

'Why Stonehouse Scouts?' demanded my father (PC 97 of the Gloucestershire Constabulary). 'Stroud is nearer. Why not them?' (Being a policeman, he was always suspicious of everybody, especially me whenever I declared that I was going to do something noble.)

'They've got a better hall and I know some of the Scouts there already.' That was true. They were in our 4th Form at Marling. But that was not the reason why I wanted to join the Stonehouse lot.

Oh no! You see, a few days before we'd had a little meeting. Old Dennis and Peter and Fatty Brown and I. Dennis had been told that the Stonehouse crowd met up quite often with (wait for it) the Stonehouse Girl Guides.

Well that completely did it. We'd noticed the Stonehouse Girl Guides on several occasions going off to their meetings and used to sit like a line of crows on a telephone wire watching them swimming and diving over at Stratford Park Lido. (Purely from a professional interest, of course. We admired their prowess at diving from the top step.)

They were rather a posh lot, those Stonehouse Guides. Mostly High School girls. We were usually too stupid to mix with them – or scared. Now, at last, opportunity knocked!

So we all joined the Stonehouse Boy Scouts and, I must admit, this time we were on our best behaviour (for obvious reasons). Mind you, we had a tough scout master – no funny larks and jokes or we were out on our necks double quick!

I must admit we had some super training out in the lovely countryside around Cashes Green in those carefree days of the 1930s. We learnt how to make fires without matches, shin up trees with ropes, make ourselves available to help old ladies across roads, and really get to know about the wild animals, flowers and trees all around us in the fields.

But we were just not getting to fraternize with those gorgeous Guides. We were allowed little social gatherings, of course, but their Guide mistress

My scouting Pewitt Patrol had a glorious week's camping here in Cranham Woods in 1938

79

made sure that it was a case of 'Jolly good meeting, wasn't it boys?' and 'I don't want any of you Scouts in that kitchen helping my girls wash up – if you please!'

We did cheer up a bit when it was announced that we were all going to spend a week camping at Cranham, if our parents agreed. (Not only did my parents agree, but hopefully asked me if there was any possibility of the week being extended to a fortnight.)

Then, it was Willy who broke the great news! There had been some frightful mix-up with the dates. The Guides were booked into the site on the same week. He had overheard the guide mistress going up the wall with our Scout master, Old Wiggins. 'Why didn't you check, Mr Wiggins? How on earth can we keep an eye on over thirty of them?'

We all sat around the Scoutroom with a look of sheer bliss on our faces. 'Gosh, don't let our Mam know', said Dennis. 'She'd have a fit. She still thinks I hate girls.' I thought I should have to be careful at home as well. Fifteen year olds were supposed to play footer and cricket in my father's eyes. He did say once, 'I don't want you walking with girls, young man, or you'll stay indoors.' So, if he got to hear that those dreadful 'pitfalls to his son's good behaviour' would be roaming around Cranham Woods when his innocent one was trying to fry up his sausages and bacon on his campfire, well, the whole trip would be cancelled.

August arrived and off we all went in great spirits to Cranham. The first thing was to pitch camp. The second was to go over and say 'Hello' to the Girl Guides. The third was to be chased off by the guide mistress. (It wasn't working out at all well.)

Then Lanky Long got a good idea. We'd try night manoeuvres. What a lark! We had some candles and a flash torch, a box of sticky cakes and chocs, and a bottle of lemonade. We knew where Sadie Long and Becky Brown's tent was. They were out on the edge of camp with some others who were more sporty than the rest. A midnight feast by candlelight with the owls hooting above us. How romantic!

Off we went that night. All was going well until that idiot Willy caught his foot in a tent peg. Of course, it would be the guide mistress' tent. Over crashed Willy with a yell and out sprang the guide mistress like a German wolfhound.

It was no good. 'Any more of this', said Scout master the next day, 'and you'll all go home.'

So, it was an 'all-male camp' I'm afraid. Well, until Friday night, when even the guide mistress thawed out. A huge bonfire and the girls came over for the last sing-song before going home the next day. Chestnuts, frying pans of sausages, bacon and eggs, chocolate cakes, sticky buns, everything had to be eaten up.

We were allowed to stay up until midnight, and the moon was up and everything was super.

The next morning I was duty man to get breakfast. The huge bonfire was now a large patch of glowing wooden embers and ash. The smell was magnificent. I set about my task with a dozen or so eggs, and rashers of bacon and loaves of bread. They fried beautifully in the pans on those hot ashes.

Very soon the hungry tribe, having washed down by the cool stream and filled their water bottles ready for brewing up tea, assembled and we all sat around and devoured our breakfast. (Fancy fetching water to drink from a stream now. We'd all be poisoned! But this was 1938, before pesticides were even heard of.)

Well, I've had breakfast in all sorts of posh hotels since, both home and abroad, but I can honestly say, *never* have I tasted a breakfast to equal that one. The taste of the food was superb, the tea brewed from fresh spring water was like nectar. The sun was peeping up over the trees and it was good to be alive at a Scout Camp in 1938.

We never mentioned the Girl Guides when we got back home. Well, there was no need to complicate things, was there?

THE NO SEX, NO SWEARING CINEMAS

Let's look back at the cinemas. Back to the days when the only four-lettered word in the cinema was 'EXIT' and the only film star who appeared on the screen without clothes on was Lassie.

In the 1930s and '40s everybody went to the cinema once a week (unless they were ill). All shows were fit for any member of the family to see. Even the horror pictures were great fun. 'Frankenstein' movies were great favourites and a 'must' for young gentlemen to take their girlfriends to, because they would cling to us brave chaps when the really creepy bits came on (and, if it was your first date, it was just the time to put your arm around the young thing and then you were away for the rest of the film).

Oh, yes! We always looked forward to the creepy films.

But, I'm leaping ahead rather, because, first of all, I must set the details out regarding the difficulties we under-14s used to have to get in very often.

You see, there were three certificates on films in the old days, 'U', 'A' and 'H'.

'U' stood for universal, which meant anybody could go in (kids and all).

'A' meant you had to be with an adult to get in.

'H' stood for horrific, which meant nobody could get in if they were under 16, with or without an adult. (The 'X' film of today just wasn't around. Indeed, there were no sex scenes in any movies, or the evil violence like there is today.)

The difficulties arrived when there was a super 'Laurel and Hardy' on, or a 'Hopalong Cassidy' cowboy ('U' certificate), together with some good gangster film with Jimmy Cagney and Humphrey Bogart in (with an 'A' certificate slapped on it). How could we young hopefuls of 12 and 13 get in?

Well, we just had to creep up beside some adult that didn't look too fierce and say, 'Please miss,' (or 'Please sir,') 'will you take me in?' (and hold out your four hot little pennies).

Some would say, 'Certainly not, the picture isn't fit for children to see.' (This would be if there was one of those scenes where the 'decent young hero' would be having a picnic with the 'decent young heroine' and then kiss her and embrace her, and then birds would fly out of trees and bushes would have the breeze whisper through them and the camera would go off for a 'nature tour' of the clouds and tree-tops!)

But there was always someone who would take us in before long and we could never see why we were not to be allowed in (unless with an adult). We always used to be bored stiff with kissing scenes and 'nature tours' of trees and clouds.

Percy, my mate, reckoned that his older sister told him that's why the film had an 'adults only' certificate, which confused us even more.

But, back to this 'going in' business. It was such a farce. You were supposed to stay with the adult who took you in, but, once inside, you said 'Thanks' and charged off to find a seat of your liking and never saw that person again.

It got even more insane when it was quite common to see a young housewife of about 23 taking in 'her youngsters' (four strapping great 14 year olds from Marling School's 3rd Form).

I spent my school years visiting the Stroud Gaumont. I always used to go once a week, and very often twice. Now the Gaumont had a most snobby way of treating the 'cheap seat' patrons! They had to go down a grotty little passage by the side of the cinema and enter in through a side door. (The 'poor class' people were the ones.) It was only sixpence to go in. But the management didn't want such 'rabble' to be seen going in through the main entrance with the shilling and shilling and sixpence customers. The manager strutted around in evening dress (if you please) in those days and bowed low to the élite, assuring them of the excellence of the programme (even if it was a real stinker).

We 3rd Formers resented this very much, so the whole mob of us hit on a first-class plan to land the best seats for fourpence. In we would go and sit in the fourpence seats at the front of the auditorium and the show would commence.

But, in the dark, there soon would be a steady stream of young hopefuls visiting the gents' toilets. Not at the same time. Oh no! Carefully planned this one was. About ten minutes between each one. The usherettes never seemed to notice what a lot of schoolboys suffered from weak bladders. Well, it was dark anyway and they were usually busy nattering or giggling with some boyfriend up at the back somewhere.

There was a chain across the gangway to separate the 'steerage' patrons from the élite. Out of the toilet would creep the fourpence-paying customers, who, somehow in the gloom, would lose their way back to their seats and step carefully over the chain into the forbidden territory of the shilling seats.

By the time the big film was due on, the whole mob of us would be well away, scattered all over the best, more comfortable seats. We got away with that for years. Nobody ever bothered to check us out.

I mentioned the usherettes just now. My goodness, they were some real beauties, and they certainly looked super in their smart uniforms, with Gaumont printed on them.

As we young gentlemen began to drift towards the age of 16, we began to take more than a passing glance at the Stroud beautiful ones and (so help me) we started to go to the boring films at times and sit at the back with a box of chocolates, to tempt them with. Then, of course, when the show was over, we were allowed to walk them home.

There's not the slightest doubt – the cinemas in the 1930s and '40s were a real centre for social (and I do mean 'social') life.

With no TV about there were cinemas all over the place. Every little town had one and the small ones used to change their programme every three days. All cinemas closed on Sundays, until the War came along, when the major ones opened for special Sunday concerts.

Stroud opened up their brand-new Ritz cinema on a rather unfortunate week – the week War was declared, in September 1939. They couldn't finish the decorating even. I went the first day it was open. It was an 'Andy Hardy' film and all the walls were just plain emulsion inside. Very austere.

But, as things settled down, this big cinema was a great draw for Stroud folk. Especially us youngsters, because the management brought in the big bands for Sunday concerts. It was beyond our wildest dreams actually to see the great names of radio and records on stage in our little town. Oscar Rabin, Lew Stone, Billy Thorburn, Harry Parry and Jack Payne were just some of the greats who played there.

But the one that brought 'em all in with dozens standing at the back was the most famous of the lot – Henry Hall – who was so famous as the regular band leader on the BBC. What a night that was!

As a matter of passing interest, the Ritz used to be where the shopping centre is now in Stroud (by the side of Woolworths).

But it was at the Ritz I came really unstuck one bright night. I used to go to Technical College twice a week in those days, in the evening, as well as a day (paid for by the firm I worked for). Now, when two particularly good films were on in the week, the only way I could see them both was to sneak off to one of them on a Tuesday evening. (That was maths night and I hated maths.) The firm never knew and the college would always accept a sudden migraine.

This particular night there was a super Bob Hope film on and I was laughing myself silly. Now, I've got a terrible laugh. (Like a donkey with laryngitis.) I could always be found around the factory I worked at because of this awful laugh of mine.

On this particular Wednesday morning (following Bob Hope), I was invited to the foreman's office. 'How's school going Tuesday night, young Jones?', he enquired. 'Great, Foreman, great', I said. 'Really getting to enjoy the old figures these days.' 'How long has Tuesday night Technical been held in the Ritz then?', he barked. 'Eh!' I gasped. 'You make sure, next time you dodge school to go to the pictures, it's not a comedy film', said Foreman.

'That guffaw of yours could be heard all over the cinema! I said to the missus "I can hear young Jones over on the left. The young perisher is supposed to be at Night School."'

'Now, clear off, and any more cinema visits when you should be at school and it's up before the gaffer for you.'

So, that was that. No more Bob Hope on Tuesdays. It was back to the maths or face a chat with the gaffer.

Now, I must have a word or two about those magnificent men who ruled the cinema entrances and the pavement outside with a rod of iron when it was 'queuing all parts'.

I well remember the one at the Cheltenham Gaumont. He had a wax moustache and military bearing (complete with gold-braided brown uniform and cap), and ruled his slaves better than any sergeant major, as they queued quietly and in an orderly fashion.

He would walk with slow and stately gait up and down the queue, and woe betide any soul who was foolish enough to stand in the road or block the pavement to passers-by.

'You there – get back on the pavement! That bus nearly had you. I thought I told you lot not to block the pavement! In line please – yes, you lot! Let that lady get by with her pram! Hey – you two girls – back of the queue if you please!'

My goodness! Woe betide also any queue jumper.

Then he would allow his flock in as seats became available. 'Two one and nines. Two only! I said two, not three. Back in the queue if you please, sir.'

What a character! All the cinemas had their mighty men outside and also the major ones had their mighty men inside as well. Yes, Cheltenham Gaumont and Gloucester Theatre 'deLuxe' had beautiful, big cinema organs, which rose up from ground level in the interval with the organist in a magnificent white suit (like a king on a throne), playing away his signature tune. (These men were famous all over the country, because they broadcast on the BBC from time to time as well.)

For twenty minutes they would belt out everything on those marvellous instruments, whilst the audience licked their ice-creams, and then the last five minutes was always a 'sing-a-long'. We'd bawl our heads off singing all the pops of the day. Then, on would come the second picture (always two big pictures in those days). Over three hours' entertainment for less than tenpence. (Not bad, eh?)

There were six cinemas in Cheltenham and six in Gloucester, right into the 1950s. They had fancy names too – the Regal, Plaza, Ritz, Essoldo. But top marks for names must go to a little cinema in Cheltenham that was not far from the Cheltenham College. It was called 'The Daffodil'.

But, my favourite was the Stonehouse Regal. It used to be by the railway bridge, where there's now a place that sells car spares.

You see, the Regal had double seats in the back row, with no arm rests in between. (We used to have to queue early to get into them, I can tell you!) The added attraction was the girls evacuated from Plymouth in the War years. We soon introduced them to the 'friendly' double seats.

I once asked my mate Lew why he went to the Regal on Thursdays and Saturdays to see the same film. He gave me a look of pity. 'My dear friend,' he explained, 'Thursdays I watch the picture – Saturdays I'm with Vera in the double seat!'

The 'Oakridge Flyer',
the 'Dudbridge Donkey' and
the 'Push and Pull'

'THE OAKRIDGE FLYER'

Every time I see a bus on a country route I am taken back into the past, to my childhood days in Bisley, near Stroud, and to the pride and joy of the Western National Bus Company that rattled over hill and wheezed down dale from Stroud to Oakridge, via Bisley, and back again to Stroud. The good citizens of Bisley in those days called it the 'Oakridge Flyer', as the good citizens of Bisley had quite a sense of humour, you see.

Those who travelled on this shaking structure of paint and metal in 1934 did so with a sense of bravery, kindled with the excitement of venturing into the unknown. One would not just say 'Cheerio' to one's family when boarding the bus to Stroud, indeed no! It was more a farewell, as if one were emigrating to a distant land.

Let's put it this way. It wasn't a case of *when* we arrived there, it was more a case of *if* we arrived there and, then again, having arrived there at Stroud after 4 grinding miles from Bisley, 2 of them downhill, could the metal beast be got well again in time for a return trip to Bisley? Four super miles, 2 of them very much uphill!

We did have timetables posted. The Western National was very optimistic in their outlook. But these timetables were a tantalizing suggestion, lines of perhaps, blobs of maybe.

Mind you, it had been known for the old 'Flyer' to arrive on time. I well recall the great day poor old Ma Brown almost got knocked over by the thing careering down the slope from The Bear, with the driver, drunk on success, and wild with surprise at the performance of his 'rattler', clinging to the wheel like a demented stage coach driver in the days of the wild and woolly West. How he missed crashing into The George at the bottom I'll

This is where we Marling School searchers for knowledge waited each morning for the 'Oakridge Flyer'

never know. We were absolutely thrilled after getting over the surprise. 'By gum!' yelled out Walt Davis. 'Here's ruddy Wells Fargo, arrived on time at last'. It was an eight days' wonder.

Now the youngsters who went to school at Stroud on the 7.50 a.m. bus would always wait hopefully for silence around that time. If the unearthly clattering din didn't awaken old Harper's cows and chickens, and set off half the village dogs in a morning hymn of praise, then they were safe. It had broken down again and, by the time the rattling, shuddering heap arrived, it was a safe bet that the young searchers for knowledge at Marling, Central and High had missed at least first period.

It was a time for rejoicing to be sure. 'Not our fault, sir.' 'The bus again, sir.' 'The bus, boy – surely not again!' 'Yes sir. It's Western National week.' 'Oh, very well – go to your place.'

The facts of transport to Bisley in 1934 will have to be explained at this point to clarify the schoolboy's excuse. You see, one week the Western National supplied wheels, while the next week saw the Red and White Bus Company on the scene.

Now this made all the difference in the world. The Red and White always arrived on time. Luxury on wheels, superb carpet, beautiful quiet heater, not one window rattling, never the bonnet about to leap up at us and no steam escaping from the front of the thing.

The driver was serene and smiling, no haggard look or jittery hands, no permanent fluttering of the left eye. Yes, there was a great difference between the two buses and woe betide any boy or girl who arrived late for school on the week that the Red and White ruled the Stroud–Oakridge route. No bus with those colours ever arrived late, or ever broke down.

Yes, people who only visited Stroud now and then took darned good care they travelled on the 'Red and White' week.

But there was one fine day when the limit was reached and to this day the old 'uns talk about it. This poor old museum piece loved by the Western National, was really trying hard and it hurt! This 2-mile hill out of Stroud to Bisley is quite a killer for the best of them. For the poor old 'National' it was the death crawl.

It was the 4.30 p.m. out of Stroud, packed out with all the young hopefuls from Marling, Central and High. Daring young housewives bravely returning to Bisley, hopeful that they would reach their destination during the week. Babies and parcels, fat old ladies and thin old men. All with one common fear – that bus!

They had reason to be fearful. The groaning, shuddering public transport got going all right from the Subscription Rooms' bus stop, made it around the bend by Alma House, changed down successfully by Henry Marriot's paper shop without mishap and roared up the last steep slope past the Co-op at a good, steady 15 m.p.h. My word, those drivers should have been awarded the George Cross for bravery beyond the call of duty. They were superb.

At the top of the town there was relief. The road levels out somewhat and for about a mile the old veteran roared along at a reckless speed, not far short of 20 m.p.h. Then, oh dear, it really starts. This awful hill! Steeper and steeper it gets and, by the time the poor old thing panted past the cemetery, it was remarked by some that it might not be such a bad idea to drive it in there and let it 'rest in peace'.

No sooner was this said, that it was as if the engine had heard, and decided to seek rest and peace in that quiet spot. There is one last 500-yard pull – up to the top, not unlike the side of the proverbial house. The gallant gentleman at the wheel changed right down and then, yes, it just had to happen. The pride of the Western National shuddered to a halt! Steam was hissing from all angles. Shuddering, rattlings and groanings, then, oh dear, no! Just a nice quiet.

'Well', said the man at the wheel. 'I told 'em one of these days this thing ain't gonna make it. "Don't talk nonsense", they said, so now perhaps they'll listen to me.'

'What about my old man's tea?' 'Ooh, Mum, shall we roll back to Stroud?'

'This wouldn't happen with the Red and White.' Mrs Brown from the farm was letting off steam. 'Disgusting I call it and we have to pay the same as when we're on a decent bus.'

'We shall miss Henry Hall, Mum.'

'My husband told me, he told me, not once, but many a time. "Rita", he said, "Rita – whatever you do – wait until Red and White week before you go to town." But I thought I knew best, now here we are, here we are – sat – just sat. And for how long I'd like to know. For how long?' Old Ma Baxter could give dear old Mrs Brown a good run when it came to vocal strength and she was just getting primed up. The best was yet to come.

'Look! I can't get the damned thing going until some of you get out,' yelled the harassed driver. 'Whatya mean – some of us get out?'

'Well, you'll have to get out, some of you bigger ones, and walk up the slope to the level and then she'll get up. There's too many people aboard.'

'Too many people', yelped Flossie White. 'What d'you think of that, Amy, too many people.' 'Perhaps they should have a notice on this thing', grinded Amy. 'Only half the seats to be filled on the Oakridge run.'

Old Walt Higgins suggested they make a bus stop there with a notice, 'Will all passengers under 30 please alight here and rejoin the transport at the top of the hill'.

But it was no use. All the schoolboys and schoolgirls and young housewives without babies had to get out and walk to the top of the hill. We all thought it was great fun, of course. Thank goodness old Ma Baxter and Mrs Brown and Amy were among the ones allowed to stay on the poor old bus. I'm sure they would have rendered that bus completely immovable if they had been turfed out to join the hiking section.

Well, after its rest, the poor old bus gave a gasp and a groan and, with a grunt of triumph, the driver got it into first and second, and away it rattled with a small passenger load inside. At the top of the hill the rest of us jumped in. With a gasp and a groan and a wheeze away went the 'Oakridge Flyer'.

Thirty minutes late, it arrived in Bisley. We ramblers missed a good half of Henry Hall and the BBC Dance Orchestra. The Western National broke all speed records that tea time. Reliable witnesses were prepared to swear that, roaring through Stancombe, it was going at well over 30 m.p.h.!

It was the end of the 'Oakridge Flyer', of course. The Red and White didn't stop cackling for months, as you can imagine. A newer and better bus was sent up and didn't break down quite so often. But the excitement was gone out of our lives.

The Bisley dogs missed it sorely and so did the searchers for knowledge at Marling School. Every man of that noble clan had to be present for morning assembly from then on. 'It's Western National week, sir', became just a pleasant memory!

The 'Dudbridge Donkey' and the 'Push and Pull'

In more civilized times than we live in these days, there was a rail link from Stonehouse to Dudbridge, Nailsworth and Stroud. Nobody rushed around on that super little line. Everybody was friendly, from station master to porter. In fact, porters actually helped passengers with their cases and bicycles and baby prams. (Now, that's hard to believe, isn't it, but it was so.)

Nowadays, the old route makes an excellent cycle and walkers' path, thanks to the thoughtfulness of the local council, and I love to get over to Ryeford (where there used to be a dream of a railway station), and walk along the old railway track towards Dudbridge. Or I go to the site of the old railway station there and meander along the old track to Nailsworth.

What memories I get as I wander past the trees and bushes and plants of every description growing beautifully everywhere, because they are just not poisoned by those dreadful pesticides that pollute so many hedges these days.

But I said memories, didn't I? Yes indeed! I can see and hear it every time I lean over one of the old railway bridges or glimpse a sight of an old railway sleeper – the old 'Dudbridge Donkey'. Yes, that was the name everybody in the district gave to the local train of one, or maybe two carriages and a fussy little engine on the front.

As youngsters we used to love to get up to Dudbridge station, or Ryeford, and watch the old 'Donkey' come in. We all wanted to be engine drivers in those days, mind you! Never to get married, but to live a long and peaceful life as an engine driver. That was it!

The driver used to blow the whistle for us and let off steam, and mesmerize us as he and his mate got their billy can full of boiling water by just hanging it in the firebox for a few seconds on the end of a long rod and then throwing in the tea. (No tea-bags in those days!) A super cup of tea in the billy-lid was the end product. Sometimes they would hand us down a lidfull.

The 'Push and Pull' went along this valley. A return ticket from Chalford to Gloucester cost 2s 6d

'Gosh', Willy said to me one day. 'I wish our Mam would make tea like this, instead of in that old teapot.' (How his mother would get a railway locomotive into her back garden to achieve this we never got round to working out!)

The name 'Dudbridge Donkey' was a tribute to the speed of the train. It had two speeds on its journey – slow and stop, especially during the blackberry season. Between Ryeford and Dudbridge are some of the best blackberries in the district. (I speak in the present, don't I? That's because these super black-berries are still there. In fact, I make a point of getting some when over there in the autumn and I'm joined by dozens of other people, I can tell you.)

Well, that 'Dudbridge Donkey' used to stop alongside those blackberry bushes. Nobody took any notice. It was always stopping. In fact, I think the

95

From Oakridge Lynch you took the 'Oakridge Flyer' to Stroud – if it arrived that is!

signalman used to have a quiet snooze and forget to drop the signal to 'all clear' at times! After all, it wasn't as if the line was full of trains all day. An occasional sheep or cow would have a wander across the line at times.

In fact, the old idiots would sometimes stop and stare at the train, as if to wonder what it was doing coming along and getting in their way. That would cause another halt.

Down to the bushes used to go the fireman to do a bit of blackberry picking. Nobody thought to complain. If they did, the guard would tell them that the signal was up for 'stop' in any case. That's if he wasn't down behind the train looking for mushrooms.

All this used to go on when old 'Donk' was taking his passengers to Stroud and Nailsworth. It was a different tale going to Stonehouse. Oh, yes! That was when they really came into their own. A blast on the whistle if a cow or sheep was on the line. No 'blackies' or mushrooms. And for why? Because they were the only link with the crack expresses that used to hurtle up the line from Devon and down from the north, stopping at the LMS station at Stonehouse, a good half-mile from the town centre.

If Stroud people wanted to get to Bristol or Birmingham, then it was the 'Dudbridge Donkey' for them. Also Bournemouth. Yes, in those days one could actually get direct to Bournemouth from Stonehouse, without changing, on the famous 'Pines Express'. (Try to get to Bournemouth today from Gloucester by train. You'll give up before you start.)

Every year my family went to Bournemouth. My word, what excitement! All down to Dudbridge to board the 'Dudbridge Donkey', snorting and panting with importance, coming in from Nailsworth with more Bournemouth passengers. Off we went with buckets and spades, cases and bags (leaping along the little line and always on time for this one). No messing about. No sleeping signalman.

The 'Pines Express' and Bournemouth. The very sound of the names was magic. Yes, our little 'Dudbridge Donkey' was part of the 1930s scene and I for one am very sad that I don't see his white plume of smoke and hear his friendly little whistle any more.

Now, as a contrast to old 'Donk', there ran between Chalford and Gloucester the old 'Push and Pull' on the GWR line that still carries the Swindon traffic. What magic for us youngsters and what comfort! A little tank engine used to pull the train one way and push it the other. The carriages were lovely and warm in the winter and cool in the summer. The guards would know almost everybody who boarded at one of the little halts along the valley.

Our particular one was Cashes Green. We would stand on the bridge and watch for the smoke as the train started from Stroud, then we would walk down to the platform and timed it so well that we would arrive as the little train came in.

'Morning, Mr White', said the housewives. 'Morning, Mrs Brown, Morning, Mrs Green. Wait a minute Mrs Arnold, I'll give you a hand with the pram! Now don't carry in that heavy case, Mrs Pearce. I'll look after that.' In they would all come, jolly and chattering like magpies.

The end of the line for the GWR 'Push and Pull' from Gloucester

'How's the cabbages coming on, Mr White?' 'Lovely, lovely thanks. Will be cutting some soon.' 'Return Gloucester – right! One and two halves.'

Ebley Halt (stop). A solitary figure is hurrying on to the path some way away. Down the long path and through two gates before the platform is reached.

Out gets Mr White, along to the engine driver. 'Hang on for a few minutes Bert. Here's Mrs Archer coming I can see.' Nobody missed the old 'Push and Pull' if they were sighted. We simply loved to ride on that train because of the lovely friendly atmosphere, where everybody cared for each other. If you got on at Chalford for Gloucester it would cost you half a crown return. Imagine that – 12$\frac{1}{2}$ p!

At a point between Stonehouse and Standish, the railway line meets the line from Bristol. But way back then they didn't meet, they ran parallel. Now, sometimes a big express would be coming up from Bristol just as our little 'Push and Pull' would be on its way to Gloucester. My word, what larks.

We would all be glued to the windows as the great race started. Side by side they would race each other. Sometimes the big LMS would draw ahead, then sometimes our little GWR would. We could see the LMS passengers all making faces at us.

Sometimes we would win. What kept us on the rails, I'll never know! Then, we would all go up to our driver and his mate at Gloucester Station and yell 'Good old Bert. We did 'em in the eye today.' 'Nice work with the coal Charlie.'

You can't have races with the LMS these days, now can you, and all for half a crown return.

Doctor, Doctor

DOCTORS WE HAVE LOVED

Passing one of the posh doctor's surgeries the other day, I couldn't help but think back to my childhood days when I used to have to go to the doctor. What a difference! No receptionists then, no nurses. Just the old Doc battling away. And those houses they used to live in. Gave one the creeps, especially if you had to go in the evening.

Long drives with bushes and trees, then up the narrow path to the flickering light announcing the fact that surgery was open.

Even in the 1950s when I came to Gloucester (a child no longer), it was still a big creepy house for me to tremble up to.

Long, gloomy corridor, I remember, and 'Which door is the waiting room for goodness sake?' People creeping about, all frightened to breathe almost.

I remember the first visit I made to this particular doctor. I'd read a couple of magazines in the waiting room and found out that the air raids had finished over London and Churchill was expected to be the next prime minister, when the bell of doom buzzed and I was off.

But, where was he? Off down the corridor I crept. I opened three doors before I finally made it. 'Tap, tap.' 'Come' (the voice of doom).

I entered and nearly bolted straight out again. There he stood by the fire warming himself, hands behind his back, dressed in dark grey, over 6 foot tall – Dracula!

A few months before I had paid a visit to the Hippodrome to see the new star, Christopher Lee, in his role as the infamous Count Dracula, and I had never seen anybody so like Lee. It was his double! His eyes bored into me. 'Well?'

I thought that was a crazy thing to say for a start. If I was well I wouldn't be there, would I?

103

I explained my symptoms to him and he waved me into a chair. Finally he moved across and sat down. At any moment I expected his fangs to be revealed. I was glad to get out. I had never visited a doctor who stood glaring at you when you entered. They are always at their desks. It was unnerving. My brother went to see him not long after and he came back full of repressed drama. 'Gosh, it's old Dracula up there,' he gasped.

Right until we left the district, we always used to say to each other, 'Well, it's a visit to "Drac" tonight', every time we had to go to him. It was uncanny.

Visits to doctors when I was a kid were much better experiences. There were some marvellous characters and, because we were down all the time with the usual measles, mumps and chickenpox, as well as numerous wheezes and sneezes, we got to know them well because of their many house visits.

At Oldland Common, not all that far from Bristol, where I was before we moved to Bisley, there was Dr Aubrey and Dr Jones (same name as us!). They were just like Dr Cameron and Dr Finley in that brilliant TV series some years ago.

Old Aubrey used to drive around in a large dated Rover, whilst young Dr Jones used to drive around in a battered old Ford. You could always tell when he was visiting around our home. There was this rattling and clanging and people would say, 'It's the doctor coming.'

When he finished his house visit he would be outside with the starting handle trying to get the Ford to spring into life again. It did sometimes almost at once, but sometimes it did not and, when I was at home ill, I would go to the bedroom window and watch with great glee poor old Doc struggling with the beast until there was an almighty roar, a couple of pops and bangs, then the whole wreck would shudder and Dr Jones would leap in quickly (flinging the starting handle into the back seat), and off he would go to entertain the next patient with a repeat performance.

He wore a long, shabby overcoat in the winter and cracked brown shoes. Mother used to feel sorry for him. He was a super doctor, friendly and very conscientious. Mother used to always have a cup of tea and a pile of sandwiches ready for him when he called to see his youthful 'measles and mumps brigade'. He used to 'wolf' the lot. Mum reckoned the poor chap was halfstarved.

There was no National Health Service then and the doctors relied on the patients paying up. Some were so poor, it took ages to get their money. They did make a little cash (dispensing their own medicines in little tubular bottles), but at a shilling a time, that didn't exactly help to buy a new coat or shoes.

One day the doctor called on a young patient who lived next door to us. Herbert was his name and he was 4 years old. Herbert was in bed with a cold on the chest, so Dr Jones was leaning over him with stethoscope in action to get on the same wavelength as the wheezing. Now, despite being young, Dr Jones was quite bald, which puzzled Herbert.

Unable to contain himself any longer, he finally blurted out, 'Mum! When's his hair gonna grow?' His mother, quite appalled at such rudeness from her offspring, apologized and Dr Jones smiled bravely at the bright little lad and patted him on the head (no doubt wishing he had a nice, thick cane handy) and that was that.

But, when the medical man had gone, Herbert was given strict instructions on how to behave on his next visit. 'You must just greet the doctor, d'you understand? No rude questions, d'you understand, child?'

Herbert, full of goodness, was ready for the doctor's next visit.

'Hello, young man', said Dr Jones. 'Hello, old cock', said Herbert. It was the end! His poor mother gave him an almighty slap and the Doc prescribed him some castor oil.

Castor oil was the medicine we always got by way of punishment. It didn't do us any harm, but it was horrible to take. But, no matter what we had wrong with us, castor oil was prescribed. Parents were obsessed with keeping their offsprings' bowels cleared out to cure all ills. Mind you, it stopped us getting imaginary pains in order to stay away from school. Even maths was better than castor oil!

A Doctor and a Bicycle

When I lived in Cashes Green, near Stroud, in the 1930s and '40s, we had for many years a doctor of great charm, who was also a man of great wit.

This was brought very much to the attention of the good folk of Stroud district in the War years when petrol was severely rationed (but not to doctors as, of course, they just had to be mobile twenty-four hours a day). Nevertheless, Dr Harrison was determined to show a good public spirit and show the rest of the world that he too could rough it with the rest of 'em.

So, to get to his surgery at Cainscross from his home surgery at Stroud, a matter of a mile and a half, he purchased a bicycle and set off one bright morning on the machine.

It so happened on that morning that my father was on point duty and nearly fell over in shock when up comes his GP dressed in a smart grey morning suit and grey hat, mounted on a strange old bike that had seen better days. He came to a halt and dismounted with great skill, and waited patiently whilst Father brought up the flow of traffic on the Gloucester Road slope. (He had come along the flat past the library, by the way.)

Then, when Dad waved him on, he mounted his old wreck of a bike and sailed past with his doctor's black bag resting on a rusty old carrier.

'Good morning, Constable Jones.' 'Good – good morning, Doctor', stammered Constable Jones. And that was that. But he did wonder just what a picture the worthy medicine man would make on appearing at his Cainscross surgery with cycle clips on his trousers instead of arriving as usual in his big black saloon.

However, Father was a great leg puller and was determined to play the Doc at his own game. Now the rule in Stroud in those days was to hold all traffic up on all three roads at different times, but never hold up the traffic coming up the steep Gloucester Street, except in an emergency. Father decided that the next morning, when the Doc appeared, there would be an emergency!

As soon as he saw the 'pedal power' approaching, up went Dad's official white-gloved arm, holding up traffic on all three roads, including the slope.

Every vehicle ground to a standstill and the white-gloved arm waved over the solitary cyclist. There was no other traffic behind him. He was all on his own.

The look of surprise on the doctor's face was something that made my father's day. However, Dr Harrison quickly recovered and pedalled sedately over the crossroads to cheers and claps from the pedestrians who had paused to watch the fascinating sight.

'Thank you, Constable Jones', he said. Then he was gone on his way to Cainscross like an Army dispatch rider, whilst Dad waved his important white-gloved arm once more and lorries, vans, buses and one or two cars, started to move, and Stroud transport came to life once more.

The Doc used to get on very well with the constable, you know. Well, he was a frequent visitor to our home, because my young brother was always going down with asthma attacks and Father was always catching severe colds due to the appalling conditions the police worked under in those days.

I can remember him coming in some days on his bike absolutely soaked to the skin and shivering with cold, and he would take off his police trousers and put them before the fire and steam would rise up from them because they were so wet. So, it was no small wonder that he had long spells off work in the winter with bronchitis.

Dr Harrison would come in and say 'Good morning, Mrs Jones. How's the patient? In bed is he?'

'I'm afraid so, Doctor. Not at all well.' 'He'll need a chat from me then.'

Up the stairs he would go and, if he came down within the half hour, it was most unusual. He took about two minutes to examine Dad, give him a certificate for another week, and about twenty-eight minutes to have a good chat about life in general.

I asked Dad once what on earth they talked about. 'Anything, son', said Dad. 'Politics, religion, the police, the traffic, lack of petrol, best crops in the garden, oh, and bicycles.' Doc was rather worried about what he would do if he got a puncture. 'Haven't a clue, constable. Should have to leave the confounded thing and walk I suppose.'

One day, when I was home, Doctor Harrison came down the stairs very amused. Mother offered him a cup of tea, which he was pleased to accept. I was there at the time and she was a little embarrassed. 'I hope the rum he has been drinking didn't annoy you doctor.' 'Ah yes, the rum! Far from it.' (He laughed this time.) 'He's had this full bottle of rum up there the last three days and there's not a drop left. He said he kept taking a nip to cure his bad chest. Now, I asked him if it had done his chest any good and he said, "Not one bit. But I've never in my life enjoyed a cold so much!"'

He shook his head, drank his tea, and was on his way once more, no doubt wondering what his strange patient would be up to next.

Dad told me that the next time he put in an appearance his chest was much better, but he didn't want to go back on those awful night patrols for a while. So, when the Doc came into the bedroom, he started breathing fast and making awful groaning noises in his chest.

Harrison looked at him. Didn't even bother to get out his stethoscope. 'All right, professor', he said. 'No need to give me the Royal Shakespeare act. I'll give you a certificate for a couple of weeks this time.' And he did.

We had some remarkable remedies for colds in the old days, mind you. Old Sam, next door to us, used to swear by a glass of cider with a poker (red hot from the fire) plunged into it. Why the poker and not just heat up the cider, goodness knows. But it had to be the poker.

It jolly well worked too. You went to bed and sweated so much on that heated cider, plus being completely blotto as well, that the cold had well-nigh gone by the next day.

Mother didn't approve of such cures. (It was a man's cure that's a certain thing.) Mother favoured goose grease on our tight chests. Or Russian tallow. Revolting stuff it was. Heated until liquid, then smacked on your chest with a huge piece of hot flannel banged on top. Didn't it just pong! My goodness, we smelled like old car engines.

But it worked. Our chests would be OK in a couple of days, and we could get out of bed and listen to Henry Hall and the BBC Dance Orchestra on the old KB wireless set.

Slow, Slow,
Quick–Quick, Slow

ALL THE GREATS ON THE 78S

O n the opposite side to the post office in Stroud, just a few yards further up, is a small shop. When in Stroud these days I often stop and look in the window at the goods displayed therein. Jackets and trousers, shirts and ties, and everything else for the well-dressed man.

But it wasn't clothing for sale in the early years of the war, or indeed for many years after. *I* don't see articles for wear when I gaze in at the window.

High Street, Stroud

I see piles of records and sheets of piano music. Yes, the old memory box is ticking over once more and I can hear the strains of Tommy Dorsey's 'Song of India', Artie Shaw's 'Begin the Beguine' and Glenn Miller's 'Chattanooga Choo-Choo'.

For this little shop used to be the 'beehive' for all the teenage 'bees' in the whole district. In they would swarm as the shop opened on Saturdays promptly at 9 a.m., from Bisley and Chalford, Nailsworth and Stonehouse, Paganhill and Randwick, and all estates and streets in Stroud itself. It was the only record shop in the district that stocked 'em all, presided over by a stern but kindly lady named Miss Grainger. This was our 'Aladdin's cave'.

Rich from our Friday night paypacket, we were in funds, and records had to be bought and played.

I had nineteen shillings and eightpence after deductions for hospital and pension. After Mother had her ten shillings, that left me nine shillings and eightpence for the cinema, *Daily Mirror*, and my weekly visit to the great Colleges of St Jims and Greyfriars, via those two popular twopenny papers *The Gem* and *The Magnet*. Now you could buy a Regal Zonophone or a Rex from Miss Grainger for a shilling, which didn't make a great hole in your nine shillings and eightpence, but that was for British bands like Joe Loss and Charlie Kunz or George Formby.

Now the trouble was that the big bands from the USA (Messrs Dorsey and Co.) were priced at two shillings and two shillings and sixpence. It was a terrible problem. I could just get away with bringing a shilling record home, but, if I was seen to creep past Father (reading his *Daily Herald* in his armchair) on my way upstairs and he noticed that the record in my grubby little hand had a white dog on the label, then there was a real scene.

'How much did you pay for that record, young man?' He already knew, the cunning old policeman (he used to drop into the record shop when on his beat), 'Good morning, Miss Grainger. Busy with the new records, eh? I expect they are getting dear now the war is on! No! What? That one with the dog on? The HMV! Two shillings and sixpence? Well, well, quite cheap!'

(Then he'd 'give me' two shillings and sixpence.) 'How much pocket money have you got left? Fourpence! You've got to get your hair cut this

My brother, with one of the records that didn't get broken at the Stroud record shop in the early 1940s

week. You're not coming to tea on Sunday with the Howards looking like a sheep dog.'

The Howards were very 'so-so', especially Muriel, all bone china and cucumber sandwiches. Mr Howard always looked like a parson on holiday. He used to gulp a lot and gaze at me through his blue-tinted spectacles like I was a thing from outer space. So I always had to be groomed like an entry for Cruft's Dog Show whenever we went to tea.

Things had never been right between Mr Howard and myself since the day he had caught me picking and eating his pet strawberries at the bottom of the garden.

'I can get a haircut at Bill Dowdeswell's,' I informed him. Bill specialized in fourpence haircuts for school-leavers with hair like sheepdogs and would also do one for nineteen shillings and eightpence a week working men.

So, despite the tight budget, one could, at times, delve into the territory of the rich and buy a big band record and be discreet with it by hiding it in the bike shed until PC 97 went on duty.

But, back at the record shop, there were piles and piles of breakable 78s to go through. Some were stacked in the shelves like the classicals and singers like Bing Crosby and Vera Lynn, but the bands were just piled in heaps on tables. Miss Grainger didn't seem to consider Messrs Dorsey, Shaw and Miller (and all) as deserving of shelf space.

Records were only released at the beginning of each month and severely rationed. First come, first served. Need I say it was something of a fight. Just like opening day at the sales.

We already knew the titles of the new releases and, like little dogs looking for favourite bones, we would lift one heavy 78 off the pile, put it down on an empty space, then another and another, until we got the treasure we wanted.

Of course, if some rascal had dodged in from school or work during the week and had already got the latest, too bad. It didn't turn up again for weeks, if at all!

As fast as you made a pile of records you didn't want, some jolly joker would be putting them back on the pile you'd just cleared! As I said just now, they were breakable 78s! It wasn't long before a very slight 'click' could be heard. We knew what that was straight away. One casualty. They wouldn't half crack easily.

Now, Miss Grainger could be right across the other side of the shop deep in some literature, but it made not the slightest difference. She had ears with 'built-in amplifiers'. 'That will be two shillings, Mr Hayward. All HMV's over there!' 'The Rex records don't bounce, Mr Jones. Put the pieces in the box when you pay your shilling. Thank you so much.'

But usually they survived and then came the worst part, getting your precious 78 home. I'd always be on my cycle and couldn't risk it being bumped about, so always cycled one-handed all the way, with the big band clutched in the other hand. A very risky business to be sure.

I can still remember the title of one that I held like that as I cycled all the way home from Cheltenham. It was a real treasure from Syd Tonge's shop, Gene Krupa's 'Leave us Leap'. As I neared my home at Cashes Green I hit a pot-hole and Gene Krupa left me and leaped all right. I picked him up in three pieces.

I wasn't well for a week after – nervous shock!

Rhythm is our Business

After war was declared in 1939 we entered into a period which has come to be known as 'the phoney war', when nothing happened. The troops were abroad, bored stiff, and thousands of children who were evacuated to the country were taken back home again by December. All entertainment was back to normal and the BBC was doing us proud. This was due to the fact that the Government had instructed them to sort themselves out, and provide the bored nation and forces abroad with the kind of entertainment that Luxembourg and Normandy had broadcast before they went off the air.

So on came *Break for Music*, *Workers' Playtime*, and great laughter shows like *ITMA*, *Hi Gang* and *Bandwagon*. But by far the most popular of the lot was *Music While you Work*, which went on long after the war had finished. This was two half-hour broadcasts at 10.30 a.m. and 3.30 p.m., Monday to Friday, of non-stop dance music, without any spoken word. Indeed, it was a strict Government instruction that no singing was to be broadcast. Nothing had to take the mind of the worker off his job in case of accidents.

So the factories were wired up with tannoy speakers and we loved it. The workers could sing if they wanted to, as long as they got on with the job.

Can you imagine hundreds of girls and fellows all bawling their heads off 'Rolling out the Barrels' and 'Run Rabbit Running' and 'Nightingale Singing in Berkeley Square', to name just a few of the songs we used to sing. It was hard to believe there was a war on.

The poor old office staff were all out of it, of course. They couldn't very well sing 'Kiss me Goodnight Sergeant Major', making up the wages, could they? (No, it was definitely a world of song for common workers in overalls!)

But, what to do when work is through? That was the problem! Dances, that was it! Live bands or records. Everybody dance! So every hall in the district was used for dances. Usually it was records in the week and a live band on Saturday nights, which we called the 'Saturday Hop'.

115

Now today a disco dance to me is a queer affair. How can you dance standing still? (They just stand and look at each other and shake about.) Dancing is what you see on the BBC's *Come Dancing* and everybody in my young days danced like they do on the 'box'. All on the move all over the dance hall.

So one *had* to learn to dance. If a chap couldn't dance he might as well go for a walk, likewise the girls. At first the dance hops used to feature girls who couldn't dance, who sat alongside the wall looking very pretty in their dance dresses and silver dance shoes, but very unhappy. They were known as 'wallflowers'. Likewise the fellows who couldn't dance. They were known as 'Brylcreme boys', all plastered-down hair and patent leather dance shoes.

On the right is Cainscross Co-Op. This is where we held our weekly 'hop' in the early 1940s

Then some bright Johnny who could dance would swan in chewing gum (like James Cagney did in the picture at the Gaumont that week) and slowly swagger along the line of girls like a farmer inspecting the animals at the local market, until he recognized one he knew who could dance.

Very politely he would say, 'May I have this dance?' The sweet young thing would say 'Of course' and away they would glide. All very civilized. At the end of the dance he would escort her back to her seat and say 'Thank you', and swagger off.

Now, if you could score three times with the same girl you were in a position to ask her if you could bring her a lemonade, for alcohol was strictly barred at all small dances. In fact, at Cainscross Co-op Hall (where most of us Cashes Green crowd used to gallop about), when the pub drinkers turned out from the pub opposite and tried to get into the dance, there were three hefty bouncers there to see that they didn't! No boozers allowed.

As a result there was hardly ever any real trouble. But, as I was saying, if you got as far as the lemonade, then it was 'Can I see you home after?'

From then on, if it was a moonlight night, and if the last waltz had been her favourite. . . Well, many a married couple in the war years started their romance at the 'Saturday Night Hop'.

But, you had to know how to dance. So that started a rash of dancing schools. Almost all of my Peewit patrol from Stonehouse Scouts decided that we should attend a dancing school. (By then tying knots, woodcraft, tracking and other fine, healthy activities for growing boys had lost their attraction.) I am sorry to report that the Peewit patrol had retired from active duty. We had abandoned the Scouts.

The fine, healthy activities for growing boys were chatting up girls from then on (and the leading chat-up centres were definitely the dance halls).

The leading dance school in the Stroud District was Miss Audrey Butt's. Audrey was a brilliant dancer and qualified teacher, very young and very good looking. Her assistant was younger and even better looking.

Bill Dowdeswell had an invasion on his hands for fourpenny haircuts and Woolworths ran out of Minora penny razor blades. You couldn't get a jar of Brylcreme anywhere! (It was under the counter in any case – severely rationed.)

The charge for an hour's dance lesson was a shilling and sixpence. Audrey taught using Victor Silvester records only. We had to stand in a line and move our feet about as instructed. First left out, right to side, left to right. Goodness knows what we were doing half the time. Slow, slow, quick–quick, slow. I must confess there was some 'horsing about', when Miss Butt was trying to get some idiot with lead in his shoes to get his steps right, and the rest of us were without supervision.

After the lads had made donkeys of themselves it was time for the girls to stop guffawing at our antics and get in line.

Then it was our turn. 'You're not playing football, Nancy.' 'I never knew you had three feet, Edna.'

But it was all good fun and it gave us all a passport to the 'Saturday Night Hop', because we were grouped together in couples for the last fifteen minutes and dancing cheek to cheek! (Even when you're learning.)

I have dozens of Victor Silvester records still. Every one is a memory, especially of Audrey Butt's School of Dancing. Yes, slow, slow, quick–quick, slow was the beginning of a great deal of happiness for me.

COME DANCING

Despite going the full course at Audrey Butt's School for Ballroom Dancing at Stroud in the early 1940s, I must confess Victor Silvester was in no danger from me as a rival.

I loved dance music and listened to it for hours right from a small boy. But my feet didn't act as they should have done once on the dance floor. Instead of 'quick–quick, slow' it was more likely I would do a 'quick, slow, quick', much to the annoyance of the young lady I would be partnering at the time. Her toes were subjected to grave assaults from my feet (the size of which had been inherited from my father, PC 97 of the Gloucestershire Constabulary).

The fact that I was a right 'kick starter' on the 'field of battle' was because I had latched on to the way I could always dance with Audrey Butt's beautiful blonde assistant. When Audrey saw that someone was holding back the progress of the class she would surge ahead with the rest and leave the 'lame duck' to the tender mercies of Sheila. I played it dumb, so that every week Miss Butt would say 'I'm sorry, Mr Jones, you'll have to stay with Sheila and practise your basic steps again. It's no use you coming into the waltz until you get the quickstep right!'

She said this as if it was some kind of punishment. I used to put on an air of deep disappointment and pretend not to notice the glares of my fellow '*Come Dancing* gentlemen'.

'You jammy git', hissed Johnny (the toilet roll storeman at work). 'Nobody else can get near Sheila with you clumping away with her.' 'Well, I can't help it if I can't dance properly', I yelped. 'Rubbish', said Gerald Baker (late patrol leader of the 'Owls', Stonehouse 1st Scouts). 'You can dance all right up in the office on the top floor.' 'What d'you mean?' 'I know, I know,' said horrible Gerald, 'up there with old Bonzo Bingham, practising your Victor Silvesters with little Nancy from the drawing office, instead of doing the rewiring.'

I was knocked out! That unspeakable idiot Bonzo had leaked the well-kept secret.

You see, we were both up on the top of the office yanking up floorboards and pulling out old wiring prior to the works electrician coming up to direct operations for rewiring. It was an ideal spot to do a good quickstep without being disturbed. But, as none of us could master Audrey Butt's lessons properly, we weren't getting far (especially after I had managed one 'quick–quick, slow' backwards and went right down into the ceiling space where we had just removed a floorboard). It was a miracle I didn't go straight through on to the typists underneath. But it was a sturdy old ceiling and held up 'against the attack' as it were.

Little Nancy from the drawing office used to come up with old blueprints for storing and take down more. She was only 15 and the junior runner – a kind of 'uppercrust dogsbody'.

We used to lie in wait for Nancy when we heard her coming up the stairs and then attempt to grab her. But she was quick off the mark and it took us twice around the whole floor area before we ran her to earth, usually around the back of the tannoy control.

The galloping around heard downstairs was put down to those noisy little fellows up there yanking up floorboards, you see.

We used to let Nancy go when we both had a big kiss off her (Hollywood style). But one day we were really depressed and didn't hurtle after her when she appeared with the ancient blueprints. Somewhat bewildered because the chase hadn't started as usual (quite frankly, between you and me, I think she enjoyed it), our little lady wanted to know why the miserable faces.

'It's the blessed turns on the corner with Audrey's quicksteps', we moaned. 'We can't get them right-no-how.' 'I know how to do them,' says our Nancy. 'I'll teach you, on one condition.' 'What's that?' 'You stop chasing me around the back of the tannoy every time I come up. Old Parker wanted to know how I got so out of breath the other day just climbing a few stairs. I said it was the dust up here!'

It was a hard contract, but we agreed, and Nancy (who was a superb ballroom dancer) used to give us our daily dancing lessons, until the works electrician wanted to know how much longer we were going to be pulling out those wires. (He'd finished making a carrier for his bicycle and wanted something to do.)

But by that time I was as good as any of the other pupils from the A.B. School. But my cover was blown by Misery Baker and I realized I would have to improve rapidly at the school or get 'done' by the gang.

So I had to relinquish the beautiful assistant. 'You have improved, young Terence', she smiled. 'You can trot off on your own now.' (But I'll always remember that marvellous smile of hers!) Of course, now the pretence was over, I found I could get back to dancing properly.

But the weekly 'strict tempo dances' began to drag after a while. Especially so, because we were getting together a good collection of swing records and wanted to show off the sounds, as it were. This was the beginning of the disco, but we didn't call it by that name. One of our crowd was a genius with amplifiers and loudspeakers. We called him 'Bomber' because his ears stuck out like a B15 bomber's wings.

He built a super, big record player and we were most thrilled when the Co-op at Cainscross allowed us to install it in their dance hall. At first we played the usual Victor Silvesters and Josephine Bradleys to keep the ball-room dancers happy.

Then we booked the hall for Wednesdays as well. But this time, never mind the 'quick–quick, slow'. It was the birth of the Cainscross Rhythm Club. I had the most swing records, so I became the club secretary.

Fed on the huge supply of American musicals showing at Stroud's two cinemas, we were soon leaping and shaking about all over the place. It was called 'Jive' and Bomber's marvellous amplifier was belting out '9.20 Special', 'Woodchoppers' Ball', 'In the Mood' etc., every Wednesday, to dozens of happy teenagers.

Thank goodness Audrey Butt didn't look in. I fear that 'slow, slow, quick–quick, slow' had become a thing of the past!

HERE WE GO ROUND THE MULBERRY BUSH

Although my friends and I lived nearer Stroud than Stonehouse in the early 1940s, it was always Stonehouse we would gallop off to to spend our leisure hours. By then we had left school and also found no great interest in healthy, manly activities, such as scouting, footer, rugby and cricket.

What we did have great interest in was activities that didn't keep us so fit as those wonderful outdoor healthy, manly activities, but nevertheless gave us a zeal for life in general and permanent grins on our faces that scouting, footer, rugby and cricket never did.

These activities for growing lads were filed under 'G' in our notebooks – Girls.

So, why Stonehouse? Well, as far as I was concerned, it was a case of what the 'eye doesn't see' (the 'eye' being my father, PC 97 of the Gloucestershire Constabulary). You see, Dad patrolled Stroud town only. Stonehouse was well away from his eagle eye, and so was I! Yes, indeed!

One of his duties was walking around Stroud in the wartime blackout shining his torch into dark shop entrances and saying, 'Come on you lot, out of there', and, like rabbits being chased by a fox, out would come three or four romantic ladies and their boyfriends.

As their average age was around 16, it was the main job of the police to see that youngsters didn't get up to moral wrongdoings under cover of complete darkness. A duty not at all appreciated by the Stroud youth, I can tell you!

Not even a streetlamp alight and 'those silly old police always chasing us'. I used to get some black looks at work sometimes. 'Your old man hooked us out of Burtons last night, Joner. He's a right nuisance! It's cold keep walking around town and I can't afford to keep taking her to the pictures.' (They were allowed to keep walking, you see. Rather like car parking I suppose. As long as you don't stop you're OK.)

Father did give me a warning once or twice. 'I trust I shall not see your face in my torchlight, my lad! Decent young people don't hang about shop doorways in the dark. Do I make myself clear?' He did, it was Stonehouse for me!

We went to the Stonehouse Village Hall Dances, which were under strict supervision by some very tough citizens. So the old Dad didn't mind me going there, especially as all my friends were there as well.

Now, what suddenly recharged our batteries was the evacuation to Stonehouse of hundreds of girls from London and Plymouth. The London girls were all civil servants and we yokels had never seen the like before. They were like film stars to us. The local girls were instantly forgotten, much to their intense annoyance. (They came into their own when the Yanks arrived a year later, however.)

The evacuated girls (bored silly with Stonehouse after London) had one thought in mind. Flirt with these local 'peasants' and, of course, the main place for such activity was the dance hall.

I remember the first one of these beautiful creatures! (I plucked up courage to ask if I could dance with her.) She looked like an understudy for Betty Grable.

When she said 'Of course' and glided around the village hall's dance floor (with me steering her like a new Austin 8 in case I damaged her), I could see all my old mates glaring at me, positively green with envy. By the time the dance finished she was smouldering on 'Regulo 9' and she frightened the life out of me.

She was about 19 and I had never been with any girls apart from Central School and High School, and the Girl Guides. This blonde 'bombshell' could probably do some guiding (but I didn't think starting a fire with two sticks and tying a clove hitch knot to a piece of tree came into it).

When the foxtrot finished I was off double quick after a breathless 'Thank you' and back to the lads. 'How'd you get on?' asked old Lanky. 'Crumbs', I said, 'she frightened me.' 'She's grown up. Leave her to the old men. 'They may be able to sort her out.'

We all steered away from those London girls after that! Proper cowards we were! Well, they were more for the lads in their 20s. (Our gang's grown-up brothers who used Gillette razor blades and got jars of Brylcreme from under the counter at Woolworths.) We decided to liven up the proceedings, as we were getting cold feet as far as the dance floor was concerned.

Now, dances in those days were much more fun than today. Top bands, like the Joe Loss Orchestra, still give the customers a lot of fun with the 'Palais Glide' and the 'Hokey-Cokey' and the 'Lambeth Walk', but most of the outfits today create a din whilst people just stand still on the same spot and wobble about.

Our village dances were much livelier than those today. There were statues dances. When the music stopped every couple had to freeze. If anybody as much as moved a hand they were counted out and had to leave the floor. This went on until only one couple was left and they got a nice prize each.

The girls usually let the side down. They got the giggles and, as soon as their bodies moved with laughing, they were out. (Well, imagine standing quite still with a man with his arm around your waist gazing at you!) We loved this one because we would rather try to make the girl move than win a prize. Tickling them between the shoulderblades usually worked well. Of course, they wouldn't speak to you for weeks after, but it was all in the game.

Then, apart from 'Hokey-Cokeys', 'Lambeth Walks' and 'Palais Glides', there was the 'Paul Jones'.

Everybody was up for this one. Even those who couldn't dance. All the girls formed a ring and walked around one way and all the lads formed a ring and walked around the other way, whilst the band played 'Here we Go Round the Mulberry Bush'.

When the music stopped, you had the female opposite you for the next dance. So it went on (and in that way people just got lots of different dance partners). But, my word, there wasn't half some cheating. If you sensed the jingle was coming to an end and, if Nancy Price, the redhead, was coming your way and, if little skinny Alan Fry (in front of you) might land up next to the beautiful one, then you'd give him an almighty shove at the last minute and you'd get our Nancy.

The spotlight dance was the one we decided to liven up one night. All lights were out for this one and only a spotlight was moving around the dancers.

When the music stopped whoever was in the spot got a prize. Of course dancing in the dark was just the job ('nuff said).

We found where the main light switch was, you see. When old Taylor switched the lights on again after the dance was over – no lights came on. We'd banged down the main switch out in the kitchen. Oh, the excitement! Never was there so much squealing and 'War whooping' in Stonehouse as that night.

The next day, Jacko's elder brother gave him a ten-shilling note to share among us. (He'd found out it was us.) 'I got a good kiss in', he beamed, 'and I'm taking her to the Ritz Friday night. Thanks to the total darkness.' 'Her?' My word, 'twas the Betty Grable one from London.

As for us younger Romeos, Plymouth was well worth a try. The girls worked in the factories and were very friendly.

The War Years

THE DAY WAR BROKE OUT

'The day war broke out my missus said to me', without doubt the most famous catchphrase of all time in this country, was, of course, the opening remark of one of our greatest comedians – Rob Wilton.

It was his most famous sketch and helped to keep everybody in Britain in those war years ticking over and having a good laugh at the same time. Together with 'It's that man again', 'Can I do you now, sir?', 'Don't forget the diver, sir', 'Hi Gang!, Hi Ben!' and dozens more laugh lines, it formed a new vocabulary for us all, because, without doubt, BBC Radio was the great morale booster all the way (at home and abroad).

But they didn't start very well on that fateful morning of 3 September (over fifty years ago). I can hardly believe it – sitting here now – that it was over fifty years ago that we all gathered around the old KB at home at 11.15 a.m. on that Sunday to hear Neville Chamberlain tell us the nation was at war.

Mind you, all of August we had been getting ready for a war. Mum had bought black-out material to put over the windows, like all the other house-wives. In fact, on 9 August there had been an ARP mock black-out in Stroud. We had all been supplied with gas masks and ration cards, and the cars had tin covers with slots in to fit over the headlights.

How the bus drivers managed was a miracle, especially on the Bisley and Randwick routes.

My gang of trusty friends were all in the Scouts at that time, Stonehouse Troop. I was patrol leader of the Peewit Patrol and old Gerald Baker was leader of the Owl Patrol. We were deadly rivals and used to try to create the best 'call-up' sound. All my mob had to make a noise like a peewit and Gerry's mob had to sound like an owl.

With the beginning of the war we were put to work filling sandbags to go against office windows should a bomb fall. This was to stop the blast blowing in the glass. (This came as a great relief to our scoutmaster, who hadn't yet recovered from the week's camp we had all been to at Cranham in August 1938.)

The major reason for his near breakdown was a complete lack of administration, resulting in Stonehouse Scouts and Stroud Girl Guides camping at the same week within 250 yards of each other! I do not intend to enter into more details now, except to mention that roll call in the camp of Stonehouse troop every night resulted in a few gaps and the Guide mistress was over every morning to protest to poor old 'Skipper' that some of her 'campfire singers' had hairy legs and had to be driven out into the dark, dark woods – when spotted!

Then we nearly drove him mad practising our 'call-ups'. Owls 'too-woo-ing' were bad enough, but my patrol loudly 'pee-weeing' was worse. 'I just cannot get my girls into a serious frame of mind to practise their knots with all this silly pee-weeing going on', protested Miss Summers. 'I'm sure the pee-wit doesn't make that suggestive noise.'

As I said, sandbag filling was a great relief for the scoutmaster of Stonehouse lst after that week's camping at Cranham.

But, back to 3 September and the BBC.

They shut down all their usual programmes at once (which didn't make much difference, because only the over 80s listened to them on Sundays in any case). But when Monday came around and there were no dance bands on the air and no variety shows – in fact no anything! – then we really got worried. We were depending on the BBC then, you see, because as soon as war was declared off the air went our great friends Radios Normandy and Luxembourg. Ninety-five per cent of the United Kingdom rather reluctantly tuned into the BBC for the first time in years – in hope! And what did they get?

Sandy MacPherson on the BBC Theatre organ. We got Sandy every hour and every day. Poor Sandy got through everything from 'In the Mood' to the '1812 Overture', then he started again. By the end of the second week a listener wrote in to the *Radio Times*: 'I could be reconciled to an air raid if, in the course of it, a bomb fell on Sandy MacPherson and his everlasting organ.'

But an even greater blow had fallen. All the cinemas were closed. In fact, everything, everywhere was closed. Only the pubs remained open. I was 16 then and, of course, too old to engage in 'Cops and Robbers', 'Pirates and Indians', etc., like I used to do. The closing of the cinemas didn't upset youngsters like my brother, but it was awful for all we elder men of the district. The little ones were already busy down on the Cashes Green canal system — Little Venice. In other words air raid shelters and trenches filled with storm water!

Now, only just open was the new Ritz Cinema, a huge place equipped for stage and films. Open only a week, then closed. We were near to tears, especially as Andy Hardy's latest picture was due to be shown any week. (Mickey Rooney's famous series were terrific box office draws at that time — all-American clean-living college gals and guys — you know the kind of stuff.)

Then there was a complete turnabout. Cinemas were allowed to open up again — just one week later! We lived again! Along to Andy Hardy at the Ritz, and, to celebrate, another dose at the Gaumont two days later for Will Hay's *Ask a Policeman*.

But, there was one big rule. All cinemas had to close at 9 p.m. Can you imagine that? What a night-life everybody was having. Not only that, but, to make matters worse, the last bus out of town was at 9.30 p.m.

Those real hard drinkers all had to be out of the pub just after 9 p.m. if they wanted to catch the bus!

And those last buses out of town. Well, how the things got away I don't know. They were packed out upstairs with a good ten standing downstairs and the platform was crowded as well. Sometimes the driver wouldn't take the bus out until they got off the platform. If he did then you could reckon on at least one falling off at the first bend around by the brewery. But there never were any serious accidents, strangely enough. Yes, from then on we lived dangerously in Stroud without any air raids.

AIR-RAID PRECAUTIONS

On the side of Selsley Hill, near Stroud (overlooking Cainscross and Cashes Green), there is quite a big dent, which looks like a natural quarry (now all covered with grass).

But people living over that way who are old enough to remember the war years know that the small quarry (for want of a better description) is in fact where a German bomber, on a certain sunny afternoon decided to drop one. (Why out there on the side of a hill no one ever found out.) Together with one dropped in a field at Eastington and some dropped at Painswick (sadly with fatal results for some folk), that was the total of the Luftwaffe's attention to Stroud.

Considering some of the weird and wonderful air raid precautions over there at that time, perhaps it was just as well. The winner, I think, was what became known as Little Venice in Cashes Green playing fields.

In their wisdom, the brainy ones had trenches dug all over our precious football pitch. We were furious. Youngsters like us didn't have a clue what air raids were all about. All we knew was that our precious football pitch was a goner. But the best was yet to come.

The idea was, should bombs start to fall, that the worthy citizens of Cashes Green had to get down to the 'Rec' and sit in the trenches until it was 'all clear'.

They were all connected together like the trenches on the Western Front in the First World War so people could move about. Now, of course, it was never going to rain again! At least, that's what Authority must have thought. Did they think about drainage? Not on your life!

But, you see, it did rain, and rain, and rain (as it always does in this marvellous climate of ours). Yes, you've guessed it! Before long we had a playing field with the best network of canals in the district.

Nothing could be done about it, though there was one of the more 'acid-mouthed' mothers who did enquire if bathing costumes were to be issued as well as gas masks. So was born Little Venice, the best play-spot the young-

It was on Selsley Hill that a bomb fell in the early 1940s. No doubt it was unloaded by a German plane after a bombing raid

sters had ever had in their lives. Duckboards (already laid in these trenches) made marvellous boats and the 'Cashes Green Navy' was born. What games they had! Crashing around, fighting battles at sea, repelling boarders, racing each other, and (best of all) getting gloriously muddy and wet.

My young brother was in the middle of that mob. By then I was a teenager and had started work in a local factory with much more important things to think about. Firewatching, for instance! Now there's a stupid title for a job. 'I'm a firewatcher.'

Actually it had nothing to do with watching the fire burning in the grate. I was part of a great team of people who had to be on duty in the factories (after working time) to sound the alarm should the Luftwaffe suddenly appear and rain down incendiary bombs on us. These didn't explode, but they did set fire to buildings very quickly, so we had to learn to grapple with them and put them in a bucket of water as soon as they landed. Why 'fire-watchers' for a name, goodness knows!

But, I'm sorry to say, in my factory it just wasn't taken seriously, proba-bly due to the fact that, when we rolled into the canteen for a demonstra-tion by the local fire brigade, the shovel head fell off the long 10-foot handle the first time and the second time the dummy bomb kept rolling off. The brave fireman (who was used to fighting real fires down at Bristol after the raids) just gave up. 'Well, you get the general idea, chaps.' (As he confided to us later on, 'Let's hope we don't get any over here. With that equipment you'd all be doing a better job than the bombers!')

So that was that. We had to take it in turns to be on duty in the works canteen from 6 p.m. to 6 a.m. the next morning. We were supplied with beds and plenty of tea, a nice, big coke stove and an HMV radiogram.

We were allowed to go to sleep, but, should the bell suddenly ring, then it was a case of 'everybody out', buckets and spades at the ready to scoop up all the incendiaries that would rain down from the skies.

Those were the instructions duly posted on the notice board. But five of the six-man squad had different ideas. At the stroke of 7 p.m. they were out of that canteen door and over to the local pub opposite, as fast as their little legs could carry them!

There they would sit supping Stroud ales and spirits until closing time, then amble back and fall on to their little beds, there to sleep the night away until 6 a.m. If there was an alarm I had to run over and tell them that the Luftwaffe intended to drop something and they would (as best they could) wobble back on duty.

But one night that bell actually went off. All was panic. Everybody was out of it, except old Henry. He was in what the novelist would call a 'drunken stupor'. But he was awake and annoyed. 'Shut that infernal thing off', he bellowed. 'I can't sleep in that row!' Funny that. It sud-denly stopped ringing. Then the phone bell rang. (Control.) 'Sorry chaps, pressed the wrong switch, instead of the light switch. Never mind! Good practice for you, what! All clear.' (That was that.) All back to bed.

But the next time we were on Henry came in with a small ladder. 'What's the ladder for, Henry?' we wanted to know. 'You'll see.'

He proceeded to climb up the ladder to the bell high up on the canteen wall and, with great care, wrapped a piece of old Army blanket around the offending 'Air Raid Warning'. 'There,' he said, 'let it ring again and I'll not be woke up next time!'

And that's how the firewatch team spent the war years at our factory. (What the other teams did I don't know.) Henry always removed the old piece of blanket the next morning before we trundled home.

But, as I said, it was just as well the Luftwaffe never gave us their attention. One team of firewatchers would have been a little late on duty, if there at all!

FACTORY TEA AND THREEPENNY BITS

The war brought great changes at the small factory where I was an apprentice. Fat Government contracts meant the management had to put its house in order. The men had to be treated like human beings for a start. Government rules said toilets had to be built and a canteen.

We lads noticed the change when the toilet rolls suddenly appeared, and we weren't required to cut up the *Radio Times* and *Daily Mirror*, thread them on a string and hang them in the toilet.

'Twas Johnny Bingham who announced the great news. 'Hey', he yelped to Jacko and I. 'Come up here and see what's arrived!' (Johnny was stores assistant.) We trundled up to the stores loft. 'Look,' said Johnny proudly, 'hundreds of 'em!' (We couldn't believe our eyes.) 'Strewth', said Jacko, 'Izal too. Gosh, our Ma can do with a couple of them.' 'You keep your thieving paws out of that box!', yelled Johnny, wacking old Jacko across the back of his neck with a tin of Harpic. 'I'm responsible for all this. Toilet rolls only issued with a chit signed by foreman.'

Jacko was peeved. 'Come on Joner,' he said. 'Miserable . . .!' (He used a word that brought Johnny's birth certificate into doubt.)

Off we went back to the maintenance shop. We had a good 'set up' there, mind you. In electrical maintenance we were surrounded by coils of cable, switches and plugs etc., in a little building away from the main factory.

We had worked hard on the two mirrors therein. One mirror (at the right angle) was positioned to look into and see anybody coming in the second mirror, sort of a periscope effect – so we could have a good sit down, out of sight of the door, and watch in the mirrors to see who was coming to the door. We could see Foreman coming about 10 yards away. It was great. We were always hard at it when he came through the door. He used to get quite upset. He couldn't figure out how we were always so busy, as he knew us only too well.

The other lads used to drop in as well on some pretence, always happy in the knowledge that the 'mirror, mirror' on the wall would tell them when the Foreman would call.

We did a useful sideline charging up batteries for the wireless sets. We made a charger and the lads used to bring in their Exides and we would ask for threepence a charge. They didn't mind. It was sixpence in town. Sometimes there was no room on the workbench to do anything for the factory because of the charging batteries. Foreman overlooked this industry. He had to! He wanted his battery charged as well!

But it was the canteen which really shook us all. The packers were appalled. Go to a canteen and sit like a lot of schoolkids and (horror upon horror) have a cup of tea from a clean cup, washed every time it was used! Never.

When it was my week I had to go around and collect all the billycans and little tins of tea and envelopes of tea and bottles of milk (medicine bottles usually) – dozens of them. Then I had to go to a repulsive old boiler bubbling away and fill all these cans with the proper amount of tea. I had to remember which packet of tea went into which billycan and which milk (what a game!). Sometimes I'd get it wrong and then I'd get a cuff around the ear.

But, up went the rules. Any man found having his meal by his filthy old lathe or drill, enjoying his toast in front of a coke fire in an old paint can, would be up before the 'beak'.

Mind you, we lads were dead chuffed with it all. No more billycans for us or clouts around the ear!

They hired a lady to serve tea from an urn and sell some awful, tasteless lardy cake. A penny each they were and the tea was a penny too. My goodness, the tea was terrible. Ivor and Perce, the packers, used to swear old Sue put bromide in it because she was a spinster and hated men. She was like the schoolmaster's wife in *Oliver Twist*. Nobody dared complain.

It just goes to show what we had to suffer in the war. We cussed old Hitler every day. But for him we shouldn't be having bromide-spiked tea.

But there were many bright spots. One was the manufacture of girls' bracelets. It wasn't long before the girls were sporting bracelets made of threepenny bits.

Now, that was the old, silver threepenny bits. New tools and better equipment were coming in fast as the weeks went by. America started their 'lease and lend', so we were getting some super machinery in. It was, therefore, easy to solder all these threepenny bits together by means of little bits of wire.

The tinsmiths were the boys for this. They did a great job with good jigs and tools to work with. The bracelets looked super and, if you wanted to make friends with a particular nice girl (who worked with another girl in the office who had a silver threepenny bit bracelet), then you had to dangle a similar article in front of her like a carrot before a donkey. The fact that it was illegal to deface a coin of the realm never seemed to enter into 'the trade'. There wasn't a threepenny piece to be had anywhere.

Another thriving trade was cigarette lighters made out of superbrass. There was talk once that the factory next to us turned out more cigarette lighters (on nightshift) than they did aircraft components.

Certainly, almost everybody sported one of these super homemade lighters in those far-off days.

People today seem to think we half-starved in the war. Nothing is further from the truth. We had far healthier food in those days. I can't recall anybody going down with food poisoning, despite the fact that mass eating was the order of the day. All over the country British Restaurants came into being. The maximum charge for soup, main meal and sweet was two shillings. A cup of tea was a penny.

We had a British Restaurant opposite our factory. There was not much meat on the menu, but unlimited helpings of potatoes, vegetables and cheese dishes. What those ladies who worked there as cooks dished up was a marvel. They could make puddings out of carrots and parsnips. Then there was the famous dried egg powder from America, which made super meals mixed with beans or tomatoes, or a bit of bacon.

Never has the nation been so healthy as it was during the war years. There's a lesson to be learned there somewhere, now isn't there?

HAIRCUTS, FISH AND CHIPS, AND ETHER

Bill Dowdeswell's barber's shop was the centre of social life in the war years. If you wanted to know if Old Man Foster was dancing all night with Jackie Green's missus at the Co-op Hall last Saturday, whilst his missus was home minding the kids, and her old man was listening in to *Music Hall* at home in his favourite armchair, then Bill's shop was the place to find out. Likewise, the ref at last Saturday's rugger home fixture needed a guide dog and all foremen at the nearest factories to the shop had unmarried mothers.

The reason why so much information and comment passed from mouth to mouth was because the peasants in overalls all had a long wait before they reached the chair. There were occasions when the war news was brought up, but, more often than not, the cartoon page of the *Daily Mirror* was the only page that was read from top to bottom. There was always a *Daily Mirror* at Bill's, which was passed around eagerly so that everybody could find out how Jane was winning the war. The *Mirror* was just eight pages long in the war years (as were all the other papers) and there were never enough at the paper shop, so haircut time was '*Mirror* time' as well.

You see, Bill was a perfectionist. None of your five-minute back and sides! No fear! Every snip of the scissors was thought out, every clip of the clippers planned. Bill didn't go in for the new-fangled electric clippers either. He used hand clippers, so the job was done carefully and properly.

Then he would stand back like an artist admiring his work, give a little cough and dive in again to attack a few more uncut hairs.

When you got the towel and mirror you might fall into the trap of thinking he had finished, but, no, he would say perhaps 'a little more off there' or 'a little more from above your ears'. When you finally got out of the chair after a good slap of Brylcreme on your nut, Bill would commence to brush you down with such care from neck to trousers that sometimes I used to wonder if he was entering me for the Cheltenham Gold Cup.

He always dressed like a hospital doctor in immaculate white coat and bow tie. If you got out of the chair inside fifteen minutes, Bill was rushing the job; probably getting near dinner time.

The lads always reckoned on a two-hour read and chat on Saturday mornings (with, say, six waiting before you, that was it!). Thus the social gathering. And all this for fourpence.

Mind you, Bill treated his regulars well with goods in short supply. Chief prize was Brylcreme. That was like gold in the war years. 'Any Brylcreme, Bill?' 'Sorry lad, only had a dozen in last week.' But he would usually whisper when you paid your fourpence, 'Drop in next Tuesday. I'll keep you one!' (I'd been going to Bill's since 1935, so I was a priority customer, you see.) You could get three Minora blades sometimes too (threepence for three). Necessary now, 'cause I had to shave twice a week.

Without doubt the most popular girls to go out with were the ones who worked in Woolworths. Everything was 'under the counter', as we used to say, and torch batteries, razor blades and Brylcreme were yours for the asking if you dated 'Miss Woolworth'. Trouble was, they could never make out whether we 'young blades' wanted them for their gorgeous selves or a Cadbury's Fruit and Nut from Woolies' sweet 'under the counter'.

It was 'Coo, ain't he lucky'. Then, 'He's going out with that girl from Woolworths who works on the hair creme counter.'

I just couldn't date the right girl. There was Barbara. She was a super looker, but she worked at the local fish and chip shop. I used to pick her up from the shop and we'd go to the pictures. But she smelt all fish and chips. I stuck it twice, but couldn't get in the mood for *Girl Crazy* and *The Desert*

Song when the aroma of cod and chips used to keep drifting over just as the big love scene was about to get going!

Then there was Linda. She was my dentist's new receptionist-cum-nurse. I fell for her from the moment she said 'Spit'.

I decided to ask her to come to the Gaumont, but she was such a 'film star type' I couldn't get round to it in the surgery. So I waited for her to come out after her day of saying 'Spit' to the patients.

I figured she would like to see the film on that week. It was *Dracula*. She accepted, much to my joy. (I expect she wanted to study old Drac's teeth.) But, do you know, she hadn't been sitting next to me for long when I thought I was in an operating theatre at the hospital. She simply reeked of ether. I began to feel sleepy. I didn't pay for a girl into the best seats to feel sleepy!

My goodness! I felt peeved! This is a waste of money! (Of course she helped with putting patients to sleep sometimes and they used ether in those days.)

It was as much as I could do to watch the thrilling adventures of the old 'neck biter'. I was glad to get out in the fresh air with her after the show. I didn't ask her out again. I changed dentists.

One of the funniest things that happened to me was with young Eileen. Now girls just couldn't get silk stockings in the war because all the silk was needed for parachutes, so the precious few pairs they had were only brought out and worn on important dates.

So, I was most pleased to note that Eileen had a super pair on for our trip to the cinema. That meant I was rated as an 'important person', you see.

Unfortunately it was a foul night, lashing down with rain, and we were glad to get into the warm foyer of Stroud's Ritz.

Of course it was the best balcony seats (used to set me back twenty-five pence for the two of us – but no expense spared with the beautiful ones on your arm).

Eileen was ahead of me and I was startled at the sight of her beautiful stockings, all white streaks. I mentioned the fact at the top of the stairs and she nearly fell apart. She hadn't been wearing silk stockings! There was some dye on the market called 'paint on stockings', or something like that, and the rain had started to wash it off. She didn't speak to me for the rest of the evening and I was peeved because I wasn't rated 'silk stocking importance' after all!

THE STROUD CYCLISTS' TOURING CLUB

'There's a chap advertising in the paper for people who would like to form a cycling club,' my old mate Tony informed me one fine day around January 1943. I was all ears. We had already bought ourselves a couple of lightweight club cycles. Father had given me ten shillings deposit to put down on a Raleigh 'Golden Arrow' from T.G. Halls in Stroud and I had to go in every Saturday morning and pay off one and sixpence until I had bought the bike for £7.

Tony regarded my 'Golden Arrow' very much the same way as the owner of a Jaguar would regard a Mini these days. He rode a super Dawes (silver and blue in colour with pencil-size rear stays and made of 531 tubing). But we were both riding around pretty well and I loved my trusty 'Golden Arrow'.

The war by then had settled down somewhat for Stroud. The drone of the German bombers overhead coming nearer and nearer then further and further away had eased off due to the RAF fighter planes' terrific battles with them. Stroud was always on the flight path for Birmingham and the Midlands you see, and it was always with a sense of relief when the droning got fainter and fainter. They always passed at night, so we never actually saw them.

The last major air raid on London had been on 10 May in 1941, and it was the war in the desert and Italy in 1943 making the news. So at home things were much quieter.

There were no restrictions on where we could roam on our cycles, except that we were not allowed to go down on to any beaches. They were mined usually and barbed wire was all over the place.

It seemed like a good idea (this cycling club). They were springing up all over the place. With hardly any cars on the road, because of severe petrol rationing, it was a cyclist's paradise.

Some bright sparks, who knew a chap, who knew another chap, who knew how to get some aircraft petrol into their tanks survived for a while, until the police wanted to know how Austin 7s could hurtle along the Cainscross Road like they were on the Brooklands Circuit. A swift move was made to colour aircraft petrol soon after and woe betide any Austin owners with coloured petrol. They were for the 'Tower' almost. A very serious offence.

So, on one fine March day, six young hopefuls in their teens, a middle-aged married man and a policeman (yes, a hard-riding young policeman named Dennis!) formed the new 'Stroud Cyclists' Touring Club'.

Policeman Dennis was a wizard with cycles. He could build one up from just the frame and repair anything, so he was our repair man. Frank (the

Members of the Stroud Cyclists' Touring Club on tour in North Devon in the 1940s. I am standing third and my brother fourth from right

middle-aged man) automatically became secretary, and our first run was to Cheltenham and back via Gloucester on 27 March 1943.

Now at this stage I must point out that at the beginning of the war all signposts were removed, so you just didn't know where you were going if you didn't know the way.

This was so that if German parachutists landed they wouldn't know how to get to Bisley if they landed at Dudbridge Coalyard.

So, as soon as we got ourselves organized for some nice long runs out into the country lanes, we were into W.H. Smiths. For what? Large-scale maps, of course! Half an inch to the mile. Everything on them (marvellous). Railways, electric pylons, rivers, airfields, docks. You name 'em, we had 'em. So, off we went with our maps in our hip pockets and – who wants a signpost!

Are you thinking along the lines that we soon were? Yes, of course you are!

Any German spies or parachutists, all nicely disguised as walkers or cyclists, had only to walk into any stationery or bookshop in the kingdom and grab one or two nice little maps, pay for them without even opening their mouths, and who needs these British signposts when we have these nice British maps?

But there was still one vital thing missing among these great cycling men of Stroud. The ladies. Oh, yes indeed! The club was getting bigger and girl-friends just were not going to spend Saturdays and Sundays stooging around on their little owns whilst their precious boyfriends belted out all over the scene to romantic highways and byways, especially when we started our hundred miles a day weekends, staying at those wonderful youth hostels.

'Are there girls at those hostels?' 'You bet!' 'Hey, what about those two from Coventry we met at Crickhowell Hostel? Coo! They were all right, specially the redhead in the green shorts!' We all growled our approval. 'I say, Norm,' I would bleat, 'did they say they were at Warwick next month?'

'Yes, and they're bringing that friend of theirs this time – the one they called "Carol the man-eater".' 'Albert, you taking the bookings for Warwick tonight?' 'You bet, in case there's no dorm spaces left.'

Me, with two reasons why I joined a cycling club, at Broome Youth Hostel in the 1940s

That did it! 'Right, we're joining. We're coming with you lot – and – we'll have our names down (if you please) Albert, for Warwick Youth Hostel.'

We were all rather taken aback, but soon recovered. 'What, on those old wrecks? You wouldn't get past Marling if we were going to the Forest of Dean!' (The girls just wobbled about on bikes with rusty chains, baskets on the handlebars and semi-flat tyres around town and that was all.)

We thought we were safe and that was where we made a very big mistake indeed. Within a month there were six girls in the club. Within a month there they were with the golden cycle wheel badge of the CTC on nice new windcheaters, club long-distance cycles that they had bought secondhand, and (what really stopped us in our tracks) cycling shorts in many colours.

They really looked super. 'Strewth,' said Tony. 'Why play away with a game going on your home ground?' But worse was to come. Those girls would go like the wind up hill and down. Through wind and rain, or blazing sun. Never a moan. They were terrific. Sometimes they would crash into a ditch or skid into a ford across a lane. We were proud of them. And do you know what? They all got married to their boyfriends during those happy days.

Certainly, as I look back down the corridor of over forty-five years of time, these were my happiest days.

OVER-SEXED, OVER-PAID, AND OVER HERE

It was whilst cycling back through Cirencester with the Club one bright summer's evening that we almost fell off our bikes. There they were. About six of them, right out of the Hollywood movies. Gorgeous-looking girls in beautiful, fawn uniforms, just standing (and sitting on a wall) looking bored stiff. It was 1942 and we were all fed on a regular diet of American movies, with those magnificent 'all-American' lads and lasses waving flags and letting the world know that Uncle Sam had decided to join the fight for freedom, such as *Star Spangled Rhythm* (the Stars naturally being American), *Private Buckaroo* and *True to the Army*. The stars were Ann Miller, the Andrews Sisters and Betty Hutton, telling us 'Don't Sit under the Apple Tree', and such great patriotic songs as 'Spangles on my Tights' and 'A Sweater, A Sarong, and a Peek-A-Boo Bang'.

The female stars were usually dressed in the uniform of the WAACS (that was the American equivalent of our ATS girls), so naturally, when we saw girls dressed the same, we skidded to a halt.

The bright letters on their uniform left us in no doubt – U.S.! Gosh, real Americans! They were the first we had ever seen. Did they eat like us and could they understand English?

We decided to try out our English wit on them.

A collection of American phrases gleaned from the movies went down like a spam sandwich. All attempts to chat them up were greeted by stony silence. We couldn't understand it. Why, in the movies they all said 'Hiya fellows, who's going to buy me a Coke?' or 'Hello handsome, what's your name?'. These stone statues had us beat. We went off like little doggies with tails between our legs.

'Perhaps our shorts put them off', mumbled Norman. We all agreed. It had been a hard, fast run that afternoon so we didn't have the girls with us and, quite frankly, we did look rather scruffy.

What we didn't know at the time (and found out later) was that the girls were all officers. Nobody without a Jag or Rolls would have even got a smile from that lot. But we had gazed at and breathed the same air as real Americans.

Yes, the GIs had arrived in the 'old country' and things would never be the same again.

Of course, it was the other way around with the British girls. Every US soldier swarmed in on them like it was their '2nd Front'. We'd never seen anything like it! The girls loved it! Here they were, in the flesh as it were. The John Waynes and Errol Flynns, Clark Gables and Robert Taylors.

Yes, the girls could hardly believe their luck and their mothers trembled and couldn't sleep at night.

The BBC were the first to realize that things would never be the same again for the arrival of the Americans in 1942 began to exert an influence over broadcasting which was far from subtle. Although Luxembourg and Normandy announcers were now with the BBC, it was all still fairly dry and impersonal (almost polite).

The Yanks were about as polite as a heart attack, so when their DJs arrived to share programmes with the BBC boys (used to announcing the gentle music of Glenn Miller, and soft tones of Vera Lynn and Bing Crosby), it soon became obvious that it was impossible for an announcer to introduce 'It Must Be Jelly, 'Cause Jam Don't Shake Like That' in the BBC-approved fashion!

Auntie's boys had to unbend, and unbend fast. We, of course, loved the slick American DJs. Let's face it, when one American announced his programme one afternoon with 'Afternoon folks. There were three bears, Momma Bear, Poppa Bear and Baby Bear, and what-ja know? They all listened in to *Duffle Bag*', it was a great step forward from 'This is the BBC *Forces Programme*. Time now for some dance music.'

Many a happy hour was spent on this lovely common on cycling runs. Tom Long's Post on Minchinhampton Common is still exactly as it was during my childhood days

One thing that did upset the GIs was our appalling British weather. As one poor soul once put it, 'You sure have some swell winters, springs, summers and falls, but – gee – I wish you didn't have 'em all on the same day!'

The Americans were mostly based at Brize Norton and always swarmed into Cheltenham. I can't remember seeing many in Gloucester, though they did get into Stroud.

By the end of the month they had spent all their money and had nothing left for taxis. (They never used common vehicles like buses.) Then they realized that perhaps cycling wouldn't be a bad idea! Now, they didn't know a thing about cycles and it was cruel the way the honest British used to flog them real old wrecks when they got their monthly allowances. Don't forget, they didn't understand our money either and would cheerfully hand over a tenner for something that squeaked and groaned, and usually had a puncture or two.

It was quite the thing to see a puzzled GI (helpless) with a flat tyre and no pump or puncture outfit. 'Say, you guys. How d'ya get air into this tyre?' Being good Club lads we used to mend their punctures for them and they were so thrilled they wanted to give us at least a £5 note.

We did play the game and kindly declined because they weren't that dumb, and guessed they had been swindled in the first place. So we got on well with the American Forces.

As soon as one of the local girls was seen going out with a Yank, that was it! We used to gather at work around 'bait time'. 'Hey! Emma White has a Yank' (like she had just become owner of a Shetland pony). 'Honest? You sure?' (Emma worked in the office and was a frightful snob.) 'Yeah! I seen her in the back of the Ritz when the lights went up. All over her he was, like he was Errol Flynn.' 'Cor, wait till her old lady finds out!' 'Nylons too!' 'Oh, that's where she got 'em from – might have guessed.'

So it went on. Any girl seen out with a Yank was a 'scarlet woman', condemned out of hand.

Mothers used to get very catty too, over the garden fences. 'That brazen little hussy of Baker's! Saw her with one of those American soldiers.' 'You didn't? How dreadful. She's only 17.' 'I told our Mildred – if I see you as much as talk to one of those Americans, I'll give you a good pasting, my girl.' So it used to go on. But there were many happy couples who got married. The 'GI brides' they called them.

There was a booklet issued to the Americans in the war (what they didn't have to do). It's a yell!

On page 2: 'If Britons sit in trains or buses without striking up conversation with you, it doesn't mean they are being haughty or unfriendly.'

On page 4: 'Britain may look a little shop-worn and grimy to you. The British people are anxious to have you know that you are not seeing their country at its best! The trains are unwashed and grimy because men and women are needed for more important work.' (I wonder what excuse they'd use for today's filthy trains?)

But, here's the best of all. On page 3: 'To say "I look like a bum" is offensive to their ears, for, to the British, this means that you look like your own backside!'